A problem well put is half-solved. The reactionary is a man of few words, well-chosen, which cut to the heart of a problem. In the history of ideas there have been works which have laid bare the problems of modernity, and whose elegance has pointed the way to their solution.

Imperium Press' Studies in Reaction series distills the essence of reactionary thought. The series presents in compact format those seminal works which need so few words to say so much about modernity.

THOMAS CARLYLE was a Scottish polymath whose influence touches fields as diverse as mathematics and social critique. Born in 1795 to Calvinists and educated at Edinburgh University, he later settled in Chelsea to pursue his literary ambitions, coming to be known as the "Sage of Chelsea". His strident prose teems with wordplay, coinages, and allusions. In it he rails against moral degeneracy, democracy, and the pretensions of "sham-aristocrats" alike, all the while affirming feudalism, the Great Man, and the achievements of the Anglo-Saxon race. A formative influence on both socialism and fascism, he was never easily characterized, but perhaps best by Walt Whitman, "never had political progressivism a foe it could more heartily respect."

THE PRESENT TIME

THOMAS
CARLYLE

PERTH
IMPERIUM PRESS
2021

Published by Imperium Press

www.imperiumpress.org

The Present Time published in *Latter-Day Pamphlets*
by Chapman and Hall 1850
The Modern Worker published in *Past and Present*
by Belford, Clarke & Co. 1843

All rights are reserved. No part of this publication may be
reproduced, stored in a retrieval system, or transmitted in any
form or by any means, electronic, mechanical, photocopying,
recording, or otherwise, without prior permission of Imperium
Press. Enquiries concerning reproduction outside the scope
of the above should be directed to Imperium Press.

First Edition

A catalogue record for this
book is available from the
National Library of Australia

ISBN 978-1-922602-02-2 Paperback
ISBN 978-1-922602-00-8 EPUB
ISBN 978-1-922602-01-5 Kindle

Imperium Press has no responsibility for the persistence or
accuracy of URLs for external or third-party Internet websites
referred to in this publication and does not guarantee that any
content on such websites is, or will remain, accurate
or appropriate.

CONTENTS

The Present Time

The Modern Worker
  I: Phenomena
  II: Gospel Of Mammonism
  III: Gospel Of Dilettantism
  IV: Happy
  V: The English
  VI: Two Centuries
  VII: Over-Production
  VIII: Unworking Aristocracy
  IX: Working Aristocracy
  X: Plugson of Undershot
  XI: Labour
  XII: Reward
  XIII: Democracy
  XIV: Sir Jabesh Windbag
  XV: Morrison Again

Glossary

THE
PRESENT TIME

The Present Time, youngest-born of Eternity, child and heir of all the Past Times with their good and evil, and parent of all the Future, is ever a 'New Era' to the thinking man; and comes with new questions and significance, however commonplace it look: to know *it*, and what it bids us do, is ever the sum of knowledge for all of us. This new Day, sent us out of Heaven, this also has its heavenly omens;—amid the bustling trivialities and loud empty noises, its silent monitions, which, if we cannot read and obey, it will not be well with us! No;—nor is there any sin more fearfully avenged on men and Nations than that same, which indeed includes and presupposes all manner of sins: the sin which our old pious fathers called 'judicial blindness;'—which we, with our light habits, may still call misinterpretation of the Time that now is; disloyalty to its real meanings and monitions, stupid disregard of these, stupid adherence active or passive to the counterfeits and mere current semblances of these. This is true of all times and days.

But in the days that are now passing-over us, even fools are arrested to ask the meaning of them; few of the generations of men have seen more impressive days. Days of endless calamity, disruption, dislocation, confusion worse confounded: if they are not days of endless hope too, then they are days of utter despair. For it is not a small hope that will suffice, the ruin being clearly, either in action or in prospect, universal. There must be a new world, if there is to be any world at all! That human things in our Europe can ever return to the old sorry routine, and proceed with any steadiness or continuance there; this small hope is not now a tenable one. These days of universal death must be days of universal newbirth, if the ruin is not to be total and final! It is a Time to make the dullest man consider; and ask himself, Whence *he* came? Whither he is bound?—A veritable 'New Era,' to the foolish as well as to the wise.

Not long ago, the world saw, with thoughtless joy which might have been very thoughtful joy, a real miracle not heretofore considered possible or conceivable in the world,—a Reforming Pope. A simple pious creature, a good country-priest, invested unexpectedly with the tiara, takes up the New Testament, declares that this henceforth shall be his rule of governing. No more finesse, chicanery, hypocrisy, or false or foul dealing of any kind: God's truth shall be spoken, God's justice shall be done, on the throne called of St. Peter: an honest Pope, Papa, or Father of Christendom, shall preside there. And such a throne of St. Peter; and such a Christendom, for an honest Papa to preside in! The European populations everywhere hailed the omen; with shouting and rejoicing, leading-articles and tar-barrels; thinking people listened with astonishment,—not with sorrow if they were faithful or wise; with awe rather as at the heralding of death, and with a joy as of victory beyond death! Something pious, grand and as if awful in that joy, revealing once more the Presence of a Divine Justice in this world. For, to such men it was very clear how this poor devoted Pope would prosper, with his New Testament in his hand. An alarming business, that of governing in the throne of St. Peter by the rule of veracity! By the rule of veracity, the so-called throne of St. Peter was openly declared, above three-hundred years ago, to be a falsity, a huge mistake, a pestilent dead carcass, which this Sun was weary of. More than three hundred years ago, the throne of St. Peter received peremptory judicial notice to quit; authentic order, registered in Heaven's chancery and since legible in the hearts of all brave men, to take itself away,—to begone, and let us have no more to do with *it* and its delusions and impious deliriums; —and it has been sitting every day since, it may depend upon it, at its own peril withal, and will have to pay exact damages yet for every day it has so sat. Law of veracity? What this Popedom had to do by the law of veracity, was to give-up its own foul galvanic life, an offence to gods and men; honestly to die, and get itself buried!

Far from this was the thing the poor Pope undertook in regard to it;—and yet, on the whole, it was essentially this too. "Reforming Pope?" said one of our acquaintance, often in those weeks, "Was there ever such a miracle? About to break-up that huge imposthume too, by 'curing' it? Turgot and Necker were nothing to this. God is great; and when a scandal is to end, brings some devoted man to take charge of it in hope, not in despair!"—But cannot he reform? asked many simple persons;—to whom our friend in grim banter would reply: "Reform a Popedom,—hardly. A wretched old kettle, ruined from top to bottom, and consisting mainly now of foul *grime* and *rust*: stop the holes of it, as your antecessors have been doing, with temporary putty, it may hang-together yet a while; begin to hammer at it, solder at it, to what you call mend and rectify it,—it will fall to sherds, as sure as rust is rust; go all into nameless dissolution,—and the fat in the fire will be a thing worth looking at, poor Pope!"——So accordingly it has proved. The poor Pope, amid felicitations and tar-barrels of various kinds, went on joyfully for a season: but he had awakened, he as no other man could do, the sleeping elements; mothers of the whirlwinds, conflagrations, earthquakes. Questions not very soluble at present, were even sages and heroes set to solve them, began everywhere with new emphasis to be asked. Questions which all official men wished, and almost hoped, to postpone till Doomsday. Doomsday itself *had* come; that was the terrible truth!—

For, sure enough, if once the law of veracity be acknowledged as the rule for human things, there will not anywhere be want of work for the reformer; in very few places do human things adhere quite closely to that law! Here was the Papa of Christendom proclaiming that such was actually the case;—whereupon all over Christendom such results as we have seen. The Sicilians, I think, were the first notable body that set-about applying this new strange rule sanctioned by the general Father; they said to themselves, We do not by the law of veracity belong to Naples and these Neapolitan Officials; we will, by favour of Heaven and the Pope, be free of these. Fighting ensued; insurrection, fiercely maintained in the Sicilian Cities; with much bloodshed, much tumult and loud noise, vociferation extending through all newspapers and countries. The effect of this, carried abroad by newspapers and rumour, was great in all places; greatest perhaps in Paris, which for sixty years past has been the City of Insurrections. The French People had plumed themselves on being, whatever else they were not, at least the chosen 'soldiers of liberty,' who took the lead of all creatures in that pursuit, at least; and had become, as their orators, editors and litterateurs diligently taught them, a People whose bayonets were sacred, a kind of Messiah People, saving a blind world in its own despite, and earning for themselves a terrestrial and even celestial glory very considerable indeed. And here were the wretched down-trodden populations of Sicily risen to rival them, and threatening to take the trade out of their hand.

No doubt of it, this hearing continually of the very Pope's glory as a Reformer, of the very Sicilians fighting divinely for liberty behind barricades,—must have bitterly aggravated the feeling of every Frenchman, as he looked around him, at home, on a Louis-Philippism which had become the scorn of all the world. "*Ichabod*; is the glory departing from us? Under the sun is nothing baser, by all accounts and evidences, than the system of repression and corruption, of shameless dishonesty and unbelief in anything but human baseness, that we now live under. The Italians, the very Pope, have become apostles of liberty, and France is——what is France!"—We know what France suddenly became in the end of February next; and by a clear enough genealogy, we can trace a considerable share in that event to the good simple Pope with the New Testament in his hand. An outbreak, or at least a radical change and even inversion of affairs hardly to be achieved without an outbreak, everybody felt was inevitable in France: but it had been universally expected that France would as usual take the initiative in that matter; and had there been no reforming Pope, no insurrectionary Sicily, France had certainly not broken-out then and so, but only afterwards and otherwise. The French explosion, not anticipated by the cunningest men there on the spot scrutinising it, burst-up unlimited, complete, defying computation or control.

Close following which, as if by sympathetic subterranean electricities, all Europe exploded, boundless, uncontrollable; and we had the year 1848, one of the most singular, disastrous, amazing, and, on the whole, humiliating years the European world ever saw. Not since the irruption of the Northern Barbarians has there been the like. Everywhere immeasurable Democracy rose monstrous, loud, blatant, inarticulate as the voice of Chaos. Everywhere the Official holy-of-holies was scandalously laid bare to dogs and the profane:—Enter, all the world, see what kind of Official holy it is. Kings everywhere, and reigning persons, stared in sudden horror, the voice of the whole world bellowing in their ear, "Begone, ye imbecile hypocrites, histrios not heroes! Off with you, off!"—and, what was peculiar and notable in this year for the first time, the Kings all made haste to go, as if exclaiming, "We *are* poor histrios, we sure enough;—did you want heroes? Don't kill us; we couldn't help it!" Not one of them turned round, and stood upon his Kingship, as upon a right he could afford to die for, or to risk his skin upon; by no manner of means. That, I say, is the alarming peculiarity at present. Democracy, on this new occasion, finds all Kings *conscious* that they are but Playactors. The miserable mortals, enacting their High Life Below Stairs, with faith only that this Universe may perhaps be all a phantasm and hypocrisis,—the truculent Constable of the Destinies suddenly enters: "Scandalous Phantasms, what do *you* here? Are 'solemnly constituted Impostors' the proper Kings of men? Did you think the Life of Man was a grimacing dance of apes? To be led always by the squeak of your paltry fiddle? Ye miserable, this Universe is not an upholstery Puppet-play, but a terrible God's Fact; and you, I think,—had not you better begone!" They fled precipitately, some of them with what we may call an exquisite ignominy,—in terror of the treadmill or worse. And everywhere the people, or the populace, take their own government upon themselves; and open 'kinglessness,' what we call *anarchy*,—how happy if it be anarchy *plus* a street-constable!—is everywhere the order of the day. Such was the history, from Baltic to Mediterranean, in Italy, France, Prussia, Austria, from end to end of Europe, in those March days of 1848. Since the destruction of the old Roman Empire by inroad of the Northern Barbarians, I have known nothing similar.

And so, then, there remained no King in Europe; no King except the Public Haranguer, haranguing on barrel-head, in leading-article; or getting himself aggregated into a National Parliament to harangue. And for about four months all France, and to a great degree all Europe, rough-ridden by every species of delirium, except happily the murderous for most part, was a weltering mob, presided over by M. de Lamartine at the Hôtel-de-Ville; a most eloquent fair-spoken literary gentleman, whom thoughtless persons took for a prophet, priest and heaven-sent evangelist, and whom a wise Yankee friend of mine discerned to be properly 'the first stump-orator in the world, standing too on the highest stump,—for the time.' A sorrowful spectacle to men of reflection, during the time he lasted, that poor M. de Lamartine; with nothing in him but melodious wind and *soft sowder*, which he and others took for something divine and not diabolic! Sad enough: the eloquent latest impersonation of Chaos-come-again; able to talk for itself, and declare persuasively that *it* is Cosmos! However, you have but to wait a little, in such cases; all balloons do and must give-up their gas in the pressure of things, and are collapsed in a sufficiently wretched manner before long.

And so in City after City, street-barricades are piled, and truculent, more or less murderous insurrection begins; populace after populace rises, King after King capitulates or absconds; and from end to end of Europe Democracy has blazed-up explosive, much higher, more irresistible and less resisted than ever before; testifying too sadly on what a bottomless volcano, or universal powder-mine of most inflammable mutinous chaotic elements, separated from us by a thin earth-rind. Society with all its arrangements and acquirements everywhere, in the present epoch, rests! The kind of persons who excite or give signal to such revolutions,—students, young men of letters, advocates, editors, hot inexperienced enthusiasts, or fierce and justly bankrupt desperadoes, acting everywhere on the discontent of the millions and blowing it into flame,—might give rise to reflections as to the character of our epoch. Never till now did young men, and almost children, take such a command in human affairs. A changed time since the word *Senior* (Seigneur, or *Elder*) was first devised to signify 'lord,' or superior;—as in all languages of men we find it to have been! Not an honourable document this either, as to the spiritual condition of our epoch. In times when men love wisdom, the old man will ever be venerable, and be venerated, and reckoned noble: in times that love something else than wisdom, and indeed have little or no wisdom, and see little or none to love, the old man will cease to be venerated;—and looking more closely, also, you will find that in fact he has ceased to be venerable, and has begun to be contemptible; a foolish *boy* still, a boy without the graces, generosities and opulent strength of young boys. In these days, what of *lordship* or leadership is still to be done, the youth must do it, not the mature or aged man; the mature man, hardened into sceptical egoism, knows no monition but that of his own frigid cautions, avarices, mean timidities; and can lead nowhither towards an object that even seems noble. But to return.

This mad state of matters will of course before long allay itself, as it has everywhere begun to do; the ordinary necessities of men's daily existence cannot comport with it, and these, whatever else is cast aside, will have their way. Some remounting,—very temporary remounting,—of the old machine, under new colours and altered forms, will probably ensue soon in most countries: the old histrionic Kings will be admitted back under conditions, under 'Constitutions,' with national Parliaments, or the like fashionable adjuncts; and everywhere the old daily life will try to begin again. But there is now no hope that such arrangements can be permanent; that they can be other than poor temporary makeshifts, which, if they try to fancy and make themselves permanent, will be displaced by new explosions recurring more speedily than last time. In such baleful oscillation, afloat as amid raging bottomless eddies and conflicting sea-currents, not steadfast as on fixed foundations, must European Society continue swaying, now disastrously tumbling, then painfully readjusting itself, at ever shorter intervals,—till once the *new* rock-basis does come to light, and the weltering deluges of mutiny, and of need to mutiny, abate again!

For universal *Democracy*, whatever we may think of it, has declared itself as an inevitable fact of the days in which we live; and he who has any chance to instruct, or lead, in his days, must begin by admitting that: new street-barricades, and new anarchies, still more scandalous if still less sanguinary, must return and again return, till governing persons everywhere know and admit that. Democracy, it may be said everywhere, is here:—for sixty years now, ever since the grand or *First* French Revolution, that fact has been terribly announced to all the world; in message after message, some of them very terrible indeed; and now at last all the world ought really to believe it. That the world does believe it; that even Kings now as good as believe it, and know, or with just terror surmise, that they are but temporary phantasm Playactors, and that Democracy is the grand, alarming, imminent and indisputable Reality: this, among the scandalous phases we witnessed in the last two years, is a phasis full of hope: a sign that we are advancing closer and closer to the very Problem itself, which it will behove us to solve or die;—that all fighting and campaigning and coalitioning in regard to the *existence* of the Problem, is hopeless and superfluous henceforth. The gods have appointed it *so*; no Pitt, nor body of Pitts or mortal creatures can appoint it otherwise. Democracy, sure enough, is here: one knows not how long it will keep hidden underground even in Russia;—and here in England, though we object to it resolutely in the form of street-barricades and insurrectionary pikes, and decidedly will not open doors to it on those terms, the tramp of its million feet is on all streets and thoroughfares, the sound of its bewildered thousandfold voice is in all writings and speakings, in all thinkings and modes and activities of men: the soul that does not now, with hope or terror, discern *it*, is not the one we address on this occasion.

What *is* Democracy; this huge inevitable Product of the Destinies, which is everywhere the portion of our Europe in these latter days? There lies the question for us. Whence comes it, this universal big black Democracy; whither tends it; what is the meaning of it? A meaning it must have, or it would not be here. If we can find the right meaning of it, we may, wisely submitting or wisely resisting and controlling, still hope to live in the midst of it; if we cannot find the right meaning, if we find only the wrong or no meaning in it, to live will not be possible!—The whole social wisdom of the Present Time is summoned, in the name of the Giver of Wisdom, to make clear to itself, and lay deeply to heart with an eye to strenuous valiant practice and effort, what the meaning of this universal revolt of the European Populations, which calls itself Democracy, and decides to continue permanent, may be.

Certainly it is a drama full of action, event fast following event; in which curiosity finds endless scope, and there are interests at stake, enough to rivet the attention of all men, simple and wise. Whereat the idle multitude lift-up their voices, gratulating, celebrating sky-high; in rhyme and prose announcement, more than plentiful, that *now* the New Era, and long-expected Year One of Perfect Human Felicity has come. Glorious and immortal people, sublime French citizens, heroic barricades; triumph of civil and religious liberty—O Heaven! one of the inevitablest private miseries, to an earnest man in such circumstances, is this multitudinous efflux of oratory and psalmody, from the universal foolish human throat; drowning for the moment all reflection whatsoever, except the sorrowful one that you are fallen in an evil, heavy-laden, long-eared age, and must resignedly bear your part in the same. The front wall of your wretched old crazy dwelling, long denounced by you to no purpose, having at last fairly folded itself over, and fallen prostrate into the street, the floors, as may happen, will still hang-on by the mere beam-ends, and coherency of old carpentry, though in a sloping direction, and depend there till certain poor rusty nails and wormeaten dove-tailings give way:—but is it cheering, in such circumstances, that the whole household burst-forth into celebrating the new joys of light and ventilation, liberty and picturesqueness of position, and thank God that now they have got a house to their mind? My dear household, cease singing and psalmodying; lay aside your fiddles, take out your work-implements, if you have any; for I can say with confidence the laws of gravitation are still active, and rusty nails, wormeaten dovetailings, and secret coherency of old carpentry are not the best basis for a household!—In the lanes of Irish cities, I have heard say, the wretched people are sometimes found living, and perilously boiling their potatoes, on such swing-floors and inclined planes hanging-on by the joist-ends; but I did not hear that they sang very much in celebration of such lodging. No, they slid gently about, sat near the back wall, and perilously boiled their potatoes, in silence for most part!—

High shouts of exultation, in every dialect, by every vehicle of speech and writing, rise from far and near over this last avatar of Democracy in 1848: and yet, to wise minds, the first aspect it presents seems rather to be one of boundless misery and sorrow. What can be more miserable than this universal hunting-out of the high dignitaries, solemn functionaries, and potent, grave and reverend signiors of the world; this stormful rising-up of the inarticulate dumb masses everywhere, against those who pretended to be speaking for them and guiding them? These guides, then, were mere blind men only pretending to see? These rulers were not ruling at all; they had merely got-on the attributes and clothes of rulers, and were surreptitiously drawing the wages, while the work remained undone? The Kings were Sham-Kings, playacting as at Drury Lane;—and what were the people withal that took them for real?

It is probably the hugest disclosure of *falsity* in human things that was ever at one time made. These reverend Dignitaries that sat amid their far-shining symbols and long-sounding long-admitted professions, were mere Impostors, then? Not a true thing they were doing, but a false thing. The story they told men was a cunningly-devised fable; the gospels they preached to them were *not* an account of man's real position in this world, but an incoherent fabrication, of dead ghosts and unborn shadows, of traditions, cants, indolences, cowardices,—a falsity of falsities, which at last *ceases* to stick together. Wilfully and against their will, these high units of mankind were cheats, then; and the low millions who believed in them were dupes,—a kind of *inverse* cheats, too, or they would not have believed in them so long. A universal *Bankruptcy of Imposture*; that may be the brief definition of it. Imposture everywhere declared once more to be contrary to Nature; nobody will change its word into an act any farther:—fallen insolvent; unable to keep its head up by these false pretences, or make its pot boil any more for the present! A more scandalous phenomenon, wide as Europe, never afflicted the face of the sun. Bankruptcy everywhere; foul ignominy, and the abomination of desolation, in all high places: odious to look upon, as the carnage of a battle-field on the morrow morning;—a massacre not of the innocents; we cannot call it a massacre of the innocents; but a universal tumbling of Impostors and of Impostures into the street!—

Such a spectacle, can we call it joyful? There is a joy in it, to the wise man too; yes, but a joy full of awe, and as it were sadder than any sorrow,—like the vision of immortality, unattainable except through death and the grave! And yet who would not, in his heart of hearts, feel piously thankful that Imposture has fallen bankrupt? By all means let it fall bankrupt; in the name of God let it do so, with whatever misery to itself and to all of us. Imposture, be it known then,—known it must and shall be,—is hateful, unendurable to God and man. Let it understand this everywhere; and swiftly make ready for departure, wherever it yet lingers; and let it learn never to return, if possible! The eternal voices, very audibly again, are speaking to proclaim this message, from side to side of the world. Not a very cheering message, but a very indispensable one.

Alas, it is sad enough that Anarchy is here; that we are not permitted to regret its being here,—for who that had, for this divine Universe, an eye which was human at all, could wish that Shams of any kind, especially that Sham-Kings should continue? No: at all costs, it is to be prayed by all men that Shams may *cease*. Good Heavens, to what depths have we got, when this to many a man seems strange! Yet strange to many a man it does seem; and to many a solid Englishman, wholesomely digesting his pudding among what are called the cultivated classes, it seems strange exceedingly; a mad ignorant notion, quite heterodox, and big with mere ruin. He has been used to decent forms long since fallen empty of meaning, to plausible modes, solemnities grown ceremonial,—what you in your iconoclast humour call shams,—all his life long; never heard that there was any harm in them, that there was any getting-on without them. Did not cotton spin itself, beef grow, and groceries and spiceries come in from the East and the West, quite comfortably by the side of shams? Kings reigned, what they were pleased to call reigning; lawyers pleaded, bishops preached, and honourable members perorated; and to crown the whole, as if it were all real and no sham there, did not scrip continue saleable, and the banker pay in bullion, or paper with a metallic basis? "The greatest sham, I have always thought, is he that would destroy shams."

Even so. To such depth have *I*, the poor knowing person of this epoch, got;—almost below the level of lowest humanity, and down towards the state of apehood and oxhood! For never till in quite recent generations was such a scandalous blasphemy quietly set forth among the sons of Adam; never before did the creature called man believe generally in his heart that lies were the rule in this Earth; that in deliberate long-established lying could there be help or salvation for him, could there be at length other than hindrance and destruction for him. O Heavyside, my solid friend, this is the sorrow of sorrows: what on earth can become of us till this accursed enchantment, the general summary and consecration of delusions, be cast forth from the heart and life of one and all! Cast forth it will be; it must, or we are tending at all moments,—whitherward I do not like to name. Alas, and the casting of it out, to what heights and what depths will it lead us, in the sad universe mostly of lies and shams and hollow phantasms (grown very ghastly now), in which, as in a safe home, we have lived this century or two! To heights and depths of social and individual *divorce* from delusions,—of 'reform' in right sacred earnest, of indispensable amendment, and stern sorrowful abrogation and order to depart,—such as cannot well be spoken at present; as dare scarcely be thought at present; which nevertheless are very inevitable, and perhaps rather imminent several of them! Truly we have a heavy task of work before us; and there is a pressing call that we should seriously begin upon it, before it tumble into an inextricable mass, in which there will be no working, but only suffering and hopelessly perishing!—

Or perhaps Democracy, which we announce as now come, will itself manage it? Democracy, once modelled into suffrages, furnished with ballot-boxes and suchlike, will itself accomplish the salutary universal change from Delusive to Real, and make a new blessed world of us by and by?—To the great mass of men, I am aware, the matter presents itself quite on this hopeful side. Democracy they consider to *be* a kind of 'Government.' The old model, formed long since, and brought to perfection in England now two hundred years ago, has proclaimed itself to all Nations as the new healing for every woe; "Set-up a Parliament," the Nations everywhere say, when the old King is detected to be a Sham-King, and hunted out or not; "set-up a Parliament; let us have suffrages, universal suffrages; and all either at once or by due degrees will be right, and a real Millennium come!" Such is their way of construing the matter.

Such, alas, is by no means my way of construing the matter; if it were, I should have had the happiness of remaining silent, and been without call to speak here. It is because the contrary of all this is deeply manifest to me, and appears to be forgotten by multitudes of my contemporaries, that I have had to undertake addressing a word to them. The contrary of all this;—and the farther I look into the roots of all this, the more hateful, ruinous and dismal does the state of mind all this could have originated in appear to me. To examine this recipe of a Parliament, how fit it is for governing Nations, nay how fit it may now be, in these new times, for governing England itself where we are used to it so long: this, too, is an alarming inquiry, to which all thinking men, and good citizens of their country, who have an ear for the small still voices and eternal intimations, across the temporary clamours and loud blaring proclamations, are now solemnly invited. Invited by the rigorous fact itself; which will one day, and that perhaps soon, demand practical decision or redecision of it from us,—with enormous penalty if we decide it wrong! I think we shall all have to consider this question, one day; better perhaps now than later, when the leisure may be less. If a Parliament, with suffrages and universal or any conceivable kind of suffrages, *is* the method, then certainly let us set about discovering the kind of suffrages, and rest no moment till we have got them. But it is possible a Parliament may not be the method! Possible the inveterate notions of the English People may have settled it as the method, and the Everlasting Laws of Nature may have settled it as not the method! Not the whole method; nor the method at all, if taken as the whole? If a Parliament with never such suffrages is *not* the method settled by this latter authority, then it will urgently behove us to become aware of that fact, and to quit such method;—we may depend upon it, however unanimous *we* be, every step taken in that direction will, by the Eternal Law of things, be a step *from* improvement, not towards it.

Not towards it, I say, if so! Unanimity of voting,—that will do nothing for us if *so*. Your ship cannot double Cape Horn by its excellent plans of voting. The ship may vote this and that, above decks and below, in the most harmonious exquisitely constitutional manner: the ship, to get round Cape Horn, will find a set of conditions already voted for, and fixed with adamantine rigour by the ancient Elemental Powers, who are entirely careless how you vote. If you can, by voting or without voting, ascertain these conditions, and valiantly conform to them, you will get round the Cape: if you cannot,—the ruffian Winds will blow you ever back again; the inexorable Icebergs, dumb privy-councillors from Chaos, will nudge you with most chaotic 'admonition;' you will be flung half-frozen on the Patagonian cliffs, or admonished into shivers by your iceberg councillors, and sent sheer down to Davy Jones, and will never get round Cape Horn at all! Unanimity on board ship;—yes indeed, the ship's crew may be very unanimous, which doubtless, for the time being, will be very comfortable to the ship's crew, and to their Phantasm

Captain if they have one: but if the tack they unanimously steer upon is guiding them into the belly of the Abyss, it will not profit them much!—Ships accordingly do not use the ballot-box at all; and they reject the Phantasm species of Captains: one wishes much some other Entities,—since all entities lie under the same rigorous set of laws,—could be brought to show as much wisdom, and sense at least of self-preservation, the *first* command of Nature. Phantasm Captains with unanimous votings: this is considered to be all the law and all the prophets, at present.

If a man could shake-out of his mind the universal noise of political doctors in this generation and in the last generation or two, and consider the matter face to face, with his own sincere intelligence looking at it, I venture to say he would find this a very extraordinary method of navigating, whether in the Straits of Magellan or the undiscovered Sea of Time. To prosper in this world, to gain felicity, victory and improvement, either for a man or a nation, there is but one thing requisite, that the man or nation can discern what the true regulations of the Universe are in regard to him and his pursuit, and can faithfully and steadfastly follow these. These will lead him to victory; whoever it may be that sets him in the way of these,—were it Russian Autocrat, Chartist Parliament, Grand Lama, Force of Public Opinion, Archbishop of Canterbury, M'Croudy the Seraphic Doctor with his Last-evangel of Political Economy,—sets him in the sure way to please the Author of this Universe, and is his friend of friends. And again, whoever does the contrary is, for a like reason, his enemy of enemies. This may be taken as fixed.

And now by what method ascertain the monition of the gods in regard to our affairs? How decipher, with best fidelity, the eternal regulation of the Universe; and read, from amid such confused embroilments of human clamour and folly, what the real Divine Message to us is? A divine message, or eternal regulation of the Universe, there verily is, in regard to every conceivable procedure and affair of man: faithfully following this, said procedure or affair will prosper, and have the whole Universe to second it, and carry it, across the fluctuating contradictions, towards a victorious goal; not following this, mistaking this, disregarding this, destruction and wreck are certain for every affair. How find it? All the world answers me, "Count heads; ask Universal Suffrage, by the ballot-boxes, and that will tell." Universal Suffrage, ballot-boxes, count of heads? Well,—I perceive we have got into strange spiritual latitudes indeed. Within the last half century or so, either the Universe or else the heads of men must have altered very much. Half a century ago, and down from Father Adam's time till then, the Universe, wherever I could hear tell of it, was wont to be of somewhat abstruse nature; by no means carrying its secret written on its face, legible to every passer-by; on the contrary, obstinately hiding its secret from all foolish, slavish, wicked, insincere persons, and partially disclosing it to the wise and noble-minded alone, whose number was not the majority in my time!

Or perhaps the chief end of man being now, in these improved epochs, to make money and spend it, his interests in the Universe have become amazingly simplified of late; capable of being voted-on with effect by almost anybody? 'To buy in the cheapest market, and sell in the dearest:' truly if that is the summary of his social duties, and the final divine-message he has to follow, we may trust him extensively to vote upon that. But if it is *not*, and never was, or can be? If the Universe will not carry on its divine bosom any commonwealth of mortals that have no higher aim,—being still 'a Temple and Hall of Doom,' not a mere Weaving-shop and Cattle-pen? If the unfathomable Universe has decided to *reject* Human Beavers pretending to be Men; and will abolish, pretty rapidly perhaps, in hideous mud-deluges, their 'markets' and them, unless they think of it?—In that case it were better to think of it: and the Democracies and Universal Suffrages, I can observe, will require to modify themselves a good deal!

Historically speaking, I believe there was no Nation that could subsist upon Democracy. Of ancient Republics, and *Demoi* and *Populi*, we have heard much; but it is now pretty well admitted to be nothing to our purpose;—a universal-suffrage republic, or a general-suffrage one, or any but a most-limited-suffrage one, never came to light, or dreamed of doing so, in ancient times. When the mass of the population were slaves, and the voters intrinsically a kind of *kings*, or men born to rule others; when the voters were *real* 'aristocrats' and manageable dependents of such,—then doubtless voting, and confused jumbling of talk and intrigue, might, without immediate destruction, or the need of a Cavaignac to intervene with cannon and sweep the streets clear of it, go on; and beautiful developments of manhood might be possible beside it, for a season. Beside it; or even, if you will, by means of it, and in virtue of it, though that is by no means so certain as is often supposed. Alas, no: the reflective constitutional mind has misgivings as to the origin of old Greek and Roman nobleness; and indeed knows not how this or any other human nobleness could well be 'originated,' or brought to pass, by voting or without voting, in this world, except by the grace of God very mainly;—and remembers, with a sigh, that of the Seven Sages themselves no fewer than three were bits of Despotic Kings, Τύραννοι, 'Tyrants' so-called (such being greatly wanted there); and that the other four were very far from Red Republicans, if of any political faith whatever! We may quit the Ancient Classical concern, and leave it to College-clubs and speculative debating-societies, in these late days.

Of the various French Republics that have been tried, or that are still on trial,—of these also it is not needful to say any word. But there is one modern instance of Democracy nearly perfect, the Republic of the United States, which has actually subsisted for threescore years or more, with immense success as is affirmed; to which many still appeal, as to a sign of hope for all nations, and a 'Model Republic.' Is not America an instance in point? Why should not all Nations subsist and flourish on Democracy, as America does?

Of America it would ill beseem any Englishman, and me perhaps as little as another, to speak unkindly, to speak *unpatriotically*, if any of us even felt so. Sure enough, America is a great, and in many respects a blessed and hopeful phenomenon. Sure enough, these hardy millions of Anglo-saxon men prove themselves worthy of their genealogy; and, with the axe and plough and hammer, if not yet with any much finer kind of implements, are triumphantly clearing-out wide spaces, seedfields for the sustenance and refuge of mankind, arenas for the future history of the world; doing, in their day and generation, a creditable and cheering feat under the sun. But as to a Model Republic, or a model anything, the wise among themselves know too well that there is nothing to be said. Nay the title hitherto to be a Commonwealth or Nation at all, among the ἔθνη ["tribes, nations"] of the world, is, strictly considered, still a thing they are but striving for, and indeed have not yet done much towards attaining. Their Constitution, such as it may be, was made here, not there;

went over with them from the Old-Puritan English workshop ready-made. Deduct what they carried with them from England ready-made,—their common English Language, and that same Constitution, or rather elixir of constitutions, their inveterate and now, as it were, inborn reverence for the Constable's Staff; two quite immense attainments, which England had to spend much blood, and valiant sweat of brow and brain, for centuries long, in achieving;—and what new elements of polity or nationhood, what noble new phasis of human arrangement, or social device worthy of Prometheus or of Epimetheus, yet comes to light in America? Cotton-crops and Indian-corn and dollars come to light; and half a world of untilled land, where populations that respect the constable can live, for the present *without* Government: this comes to light; and the profound sorrow of all nobler hearts, here uttering itself as silent patient unspeakable ennui, there coming out as vague elegiac wailings, that there is still next to nothing more. 'Anarchy *plus* a street-constable:' that also is anarchic to me, and other than quite lovely!

I foresee, too, that, long before the waste lands are full, the very street-constable, on these poor terms, will have become impossible: without the waste lands, as here in our Europe, I do not see how he could continue possible many weeks. Cease to brag to me of America, and its model institutions and constitutions. To men in their sleep there is nothing granted in this world: nothing, or as good as nothing, to men that sit idly *caucusing* and ballot-boxing on the graves of their heroic ancestors, saying, "It is well, it is well!" Corn and bacon are granted: not a very sublime boon, on such conditions; a boon moreover which, on such conditions, cannot last! No: America too will have to strain its energies, in quite other fashion than this; to crack its sinews, and all-but break its heart, as the rest of us have had to do, in thousandfold wrestle with the Pythons and mud-demons, before it can become a habitation for the gods. America's battle is yet to fight; and we, sorrowful though nothing doubting, will wish her strength for it. New Spiritual Pythons, plenty of them; enormous Megatherions, as ugly as were ever born of mud, loom huge and hideous out of the twilight Future on America; and she will have her own agony, and her own victory, but on other terms than she is yet quite aware of. Hitherto she but ploughs and hammers, in a very successful manner; hitherto, in spite of her 'roast-goose with apple-sauce,' she is not much. 'Roast-goose with apple-sauce for the poorest working-man:' well, surely that is something,—thanks to your respect for the street-constable, and to your continents of fertile waste land;—but that, even if it could continue, is by no means enough; that is not even an instalment towards what will be required of you. My friend, brag not yet of our American cousins! Their quantity of cotton, dollars, industry and resources, I believe to be almost unspeakable; but I can by no means worship the like of these. What great human soul, what great thought, what great noble thing that one could worship, or loyally admire, has yet been produced there? None: the American cousins have yet done none of these things. "What they have done?" growls Smelfungus, tired of the subject: "They have doubled their population every twenty years. They have begotten, with a rapidity beyond recorded example, Eighteen Millions of the greatest *bores* ever seen in this world before,—that hitherto is their feat in History!"—And so we leave them, for the present; and cannot predict the success of Democracy, on this side of the Atlantic, from their example.

Alas, on this side of the Atlantic and on that, Democracy, we apprehend, is forever impossible! So much, with certainty of loud astonished contradiction from all manner of men at present, but with sure appeal to the Law of Nature and the ever-abiding Fact, may be suggested and asserted once more. The Universe itself is a Monarchy and Hierarchy; large liberty of 'voting' there, all manner of choice, utmost free-will, but with conditions inexorable and immeasurable annexed to every exercise of the same. A most free commonwealth of 'voters;' but with Eternal Justice to preside over it, Eternal Justice enforced by Almighty Power! This is the model of 'constitutions;' this: nor in any Nation where there has not yet (in some supportable and withal some constantly-increasing degree) been confided to the *Noblest*, with his select series of *Nobler*, the divine everlasting duty of directing and controlling the Ignoble, has the 'Kingdom of God,' which we all pray for, 'come,' nor can 'His will' even *tend* to be 'done on Earth as it is in Heaven' till then. My Christian friends, and indeed my Sham-Christian and Anti-Christian, and all manner of men, are invited to reflect on this. They will find it to be the truth of the case. The Noble in the high place, the Ignoble in the low; that is, in all times and in all countries, the

The Present Time

Almighty Maker's Law.

To raise the Sham-Noblest, and solemnly consecrate *him* by whatever method, new-devised, or slavishly adhered to from old wont, this, little as we may regard it, is, in all times and countries, a practical blasphemy, and Nature will in no wise forget it. Alas, there lies the origin, the fatal necessity, of modern Democracy everywhere. It is the Noblest, not the Sham-Noblest; it is God-Almighty's Noble, not the Court-Tailor's Noble, nor the Able-Editor's Noble, that must in some approximate degree, be raised to the supreme place; he and not a counterfeit,—under penalties! Penalties deep as death, and at length terrible as hell-on-earth, my constitutional friend!—Will the ballot-box raise the Noblest to the chief place; does any sane man deliberately believe such a thing? That nevertheless is the indispensable result, attain it how we may: if that is attained, all is attained; if not that, nothing. He that cannot believe the ballot-box to be attaining it, will be comparatively indifferent to the ballot-box. Excellent for keeping the ship's crew at peace under their Phantasm Captain; but unserviceable, under such, for getting round Cape Horn. Alas, that there should be human beings requiring to have these things argued of, at this late time of day!

I say, it is the everlasting privilege of the foolish to be governed by the wise; to be guided in the right path by those who know it better than they. This is the first 'right of man;' compared with which all other rights are as nothing,—mere superfluities, corollaries which will follow of their own accord out of this; if they be not contradictions to this, and less than nothing! To the wise it is not a privilege; far other indeed. Doubtless, as bringing preservation to their country, it implies preservation of themselves withal; but intrinsically it is the harshest duty a wise man, if he be indeed wise, has laid to his hand. A duty which he would fain enough shirk; which accordingly, in these sad times of doubt and cowardly sloth, he has long everywhere been endeavouring to reduce to its minimum, and has in fact in most cases nearly escaped altogether. It is an ungoverned world; a world which we flatter ourselves will henceforth need no governing. On the dust of our heroic ancestors we too sit ballot-boxing, saying to one another, It is well, it is well! By inheritance of their noble struggles, we have been permitted to sit slothful so long. By noble toil, not by shallow laughter and vain talk, they made this English Existence from a savage forest into an arable inhabitable field for us; and we, idly dreaming it would grow spontaneous crops forever,—find it now in a too questionable state; peremptorily requiring real labour and agriculture again. Real 'agriculture' is not pleasant; much pleasanter to reap and winnow (with ballot-box or otherwise) than to plough!

Who would govern that can get along without governing? He that is fittest for it, is of all men the unwillingest unless constrained. By multifarious devices we have been endeavouring to dispense with governing; and by very superficial speculations, of *laissez-faire*, supply-and-demand, &c. &c. to persuade ourselves that it is best so. The Real Captain, unless it be some Captain of mechanical Industry hired by Mammon, where is he in these days? Most likely, in silence, in sad isolation somewhere, in remote obscurity; trying if, in an evil ungoverned time, he cannot at least govern himself. The Real Captain undiscoverable; the Phantasm Captain everywhere very conspicuous:—it is thought Phantasm Captains, aided by ballot-boxes, are the true method, after all. They are much the pleasantest for the time being! And so no *Dux* or Duke of any sort, in any province of our affairs, now *leads*: the Duke's Bailiff *leads*, what little leading is required for getting-in the rents; and the Duke merely rides in the state-coach. It is everywhere so: and now at last we see a world all rushing towards strange consummations, because it is and has long been so!

I do not suppose any reader of mine, or many persons in England at all, have much faith in Fraternity, Equality and the Revolutionary Millenniums preached by the French Prophets in this age: but there are many movements here too which tend inevitably in the like direction; and good men, who would stand aghast at Red Republic and its adjuncts, seem to me travelling at full speed towards that or a similar goal! Certainly the notion everywhere prevails among us too, and preaches itself abroad in every dialect, uncontradicted anywhere so far as I can hear, That the grand panacea for social woes is what we call 'enfranchisement,' 'emancipation;' or, translated into practical language, the cutting asunder of human relations, wherever they are found grievous, as is like to be pretty universally the case at the rate we have been going for some generations past. Let us all be 'free' of one another; we shall then be happy. Free, without bond or connection except that of cash-payment; fair day's wages for the fair day's work; bargained for by voluntary contract, and law of supply-and-demand: this is thought to be the true solution of all difficulties and injustices that have occurred between man and man.

To rectify the relation that exists between two men, is there no method, then, but that of ending it? The old relation has become unsuitable, obsolete, perhaps unjust; it imperatively requires to be amended; and the remedy is, Abolish it, let there henceforth be no relation at all. From the 'Sacrament of Marriage' downwards, human beings used to be manifoldly related, one to another, and each to all; and there was no relation among human beings, just or unjust, that had not its grievances and difficulties, its necessities on both sides to bear and forbear. But henceforth, be it known, we have changed all that, by favour of Heaven: 'the voluntary principle' has come-up, which will itself do the business for us; and now let a new Sacrament, that of *Divorce*, which we call emancipation, and spout-of on our platforms, be universally the order of the day!—Have men considered whither all this is tending, and what it certainly enough betokens? Cut every human relation which has anywhere grown uneasy sheer asunder; reduce whatsoever was compulsory to voluntary, whatsoever was permanent among us to the condition of nomadic:—in other words, loosen by assiduous wedges in every joint, the whole fabric of social existence, stone from stone; till at last, all now being loose enough, it can, as we already see in most countries, be overset by sudden outburst of revolutionary rage; and, lying as mere mountains of anarchic rubbish, solicit you to sing Fraternity &c. over it, and to rejoice in the new remarkable era of human progress we have arrived at.

Certainly Emancipation proceeds with rapid strides among us, this good while; and has got to such a length as might give rise to reflections in men of a serious turn. West-Indian Blacks are emancipated, and it appears refuse to work: Irish Whites have long been entirely emancipated; and nobody asks them to work, or on condition of finding them potatoes (which, of course, is indispensable), permits them to work.— Among speculative persons, a question has sometimes risen:

Carlyle

In the progress of Emancipation, are we to look for a time when all the Horses also are to be emancipated, and brought to the supply-and-demand principle? Horses too have 'motives;' are acted-on by hunger, fear, hope, love of oats, terror of platted leather; nay they have vanity, ambition, emulation, thankfulness, vindictiveness; some rude outline of all our human spiritualities,—a rude resemblance to us in mind and intelligence, even as they have in bodily frame. The Horse, poor dumb four-footed fellow, he too has his private feelings, his affections, gratitudes; and deserves good usage; no human master, without crime, shall treat him unjustly either, or recklessly lay-on the whip where it is not needed:—I am sure if I could make him 'happy,' I should be willing to grant a small vote (in addition to the late twenty millions) for that object!

Him too you occasionally tyrannise over; and with bad result to yourselves, among others; using the leather in a tyrannous unnecessary manner; withholding, or scantily furnishing, the oats and ventilated stabling that are due. Rugged horse-subduers, one fears they are a little tyrannous at times. "Am I not a horse, and *half*-brother?"—To remedy which, so far as remediable, fancy—the horses all 'emancipated;' restored to their primeval right of property in the grass of this Globe: turned-out to graze in an independent supply-and-demand manner! So long as grass lasts, I dare say they are very happy, or think themselves so. And Farmer Hodge sallying forth, on a dry spring morning, with a sieve of oats in his hand, and agony of eager expectation in his heart, is he happy? Help me to plough this day, Black Dobbin: oats in full measure if thou wilt. "Hlunh, No—thank!" snorts Black Dobbin; he prefers glorious liberty and the grass. Bay Darby, wilt not thou perhaps? "Hlunh!"—Gray Joan, then, my beautiful broad-bottomed mare,—O Heaven, she too answers Hlunh! Not a quadruped of them will plough a stroke for me. Corn-crops are *ended* in this world!—For the sake, if not of Hodge, then of Hodge's horses, one prays this benevolent practice might now cease, and a new and better one try to begin. Small kindness to Hodge's horses to emancipate them! The fate of all emancipated horses is, sooner or later, inevitable. To have in this habitable Earth no grass to eat,—in Black Jamaica gradually none, as in White Connemara already none;—to roam aimless, wasting the seed-fields of the world; and be hunted home to Chaos, by the due watch-dogs and due hell-dogs, with such horrors of forsaken wretchedness as were never seen before! These things are not sport; they are terribly true, in this country at this hour.

Between our Black West Indies and our White Ireland, between these two extremes of lazy refusal to work, and of famishing inability to find any work, what a world have we made of it, with our fierce Mammon-worships, and our benevolent philanderings, and idle godless nonsenses of one kind and another! Supply-and-demand, Leave-it-alone, Voluntary Principle, Time will mend it:—till British industrial existence seems fast becoming one huge poison-swamp of reeking pestilence physical and moral; a hideous *living* Golgotha of souls and bodies buried alive; such a Curtius' gulf, communicating with the Nether Deeps, as the Sun never saw till now. These scenes, which the *Morning Chronicle* is bringing home to all minds of men,—thanks to it for a service such as Newspapers have seldom done,—ought to excite unspeakable reflections in every mind. Thirty-thousand outcast Needlewomen working themselves swiftly to death; three-million Paupers rotting in forced idleness, *helping* said Needlewomen to die: these are but items in the sad ledger of despair.

Thirty-thousand wretched women, sunk in that putrefying well of abominations; they have oozed-in upon London, from the universal Stygian quagmire of British industrial life; are accumulated in the *well* of the concern, to that extent. British charity is smitten to the heart, at the laying-bare of such a scene; passionately undertakes, by enormous subscription of money, or by other enormous effort, to redress that individual horror; as I and all men hope it may. But, alas, what next? This general well and cesspool once baled clean out today, will begin before night to fill itself anew. The universal Stygian quagmire is still there; opulent in women ready to be ruined, and in men ready. Towards the same sad cesspool will these waste currents of human ruin ooze and gravitate as heretofore; except in draining the universal quagmire itself there is no remedy. "And for that, what is the method?" cry many in an angry manner. To whom, for the present, I answer only, "Not 'emancipation,' it would seem, my friends; not the cutting-loose of human ties, something far the reverse of that!"

Many things have been written about shirtmaking; but here perhaps is the saddest thing of all, not written anywhere till now, that I know of. Shirts by the thirty-thousand are made at twopence-halfpenny each;—and in the mean while no needlewoman, distressed or other, can be procured in London by any housewife to give, for fair wages, fair help in sewing. Ask any thrifty house-mother, high or low, and she will answer. In high houses and in low, there is the same answer: no *real* needlewoman, 'distressed' or other, has been found attainable in any of the houses I frequent. Imaginary needle-women, who demand considerable wages, and have a deepish appetite for beer and viands, I hear of everywhere; but their sewing proves too often a distracted puckering and botching; not sewing, only the fallacious hope of it, a fond imagination of the mind. Good sempstresses are to be hired in every village; and in London, with its famishing thirty-thousand, not at all, or hardly.—Is not No-government beautiful in human business? To such length has the Leave-alone principle carried it, by way of organising labour, in this affair of shirtmaking. Let us hope the Leave-alone principle has now got its apotheosis; and taken wing towards higher regions than ours, to deal henceforth with a class of affairs more appropriate for it!

Reader, did you ever hear of 'Constituted Anarchy'? Anarchy; the choking, sweltering, deadly and killing rule of No-rule; the consecration of cupidity, and braying folly, and dim stupidity and baseness, in most of the affairs of men? Slop-shirts attainable three-halfpence cheaper, by the ruin of living bodies and immortal souls? Solemn Bishops and high Dignitaries, *our* divine 'Pillars of Fire by night,' debating meanwhile, with their largest wigs and gravest look, upon something they call 'prevenient grace'? Alas, our noble men of genius, Heaven's *real* messengers to us, they also rendered nearly futile by the wasteful time;—preappointed they everywhere, and assiduously trained by all their pedagogues and monitors, to 'rise in Parliament,' to compose orations, write books, or in short speak *words*, for the approval of reviewers; instead of doing real kingly *work* to be approved of by the gods! Our 'Government,' a highly 'responsible' one; responsible to no God that I can hear of, but to the twenty-seven million *gods* of the shilling gallery. A Government tumbling and drifting on the whirlpools and mud-deluges, floating atop in a conspicuous manner, no-whither,—like the carcass of a drowned ass. Authentic *Chaos* come up into this sunny Cosmos again; and all men singing *Gloria in excelsis* to it. In spirituals and temporals, in field and workshop, from Manchester to Dorsetshire, from Lambeth Palace to the Lanes of Whitechapel, wherever men meet and toil and traffic together,—Anarchy, Anarchy; and only the street-constable (though with ever-increasing difficulty) still maintaining himself in the middle of it; that so, for one thing, this blessed exchange of slop-shirts for the souls of women may transact itself in a peaceable manner!—I, for my part, do profess myself in eternal opposition to this, and discern well that universal Ruin has us in the wind, unless we can get out of this. My friend Crabbe, in a late number of his *Intermittent Radiator*, pertinently enough exclaims:

'When shall we have done with all this of British Liberty, Voluntary Principle, Dangers of Centralisation, and the like? It is really getting too bad. For British Liberty, it seems, the people cannot be taught to read. British Liberty, shuddering to interfere with the rights of capital, takes six or eight millions of money annually to feed the idle labourer whom it dare not employ. For British Liberty we live over poisonous cesspools, gully-drains, and detestable abominations; and omnipotent London cannot sweep the dirt out of itself. British Liberty produces—what? Floods of Hansard Debates every year, and apparently little else at present. If these are the results of British Liberty, I, for one, move we should lay it on the shelf a little, and look-out for something other and farther. We have achieved British Liberty hundreds of years ago; and are fast growing, on the strength of it, one of the most absurd populations the Sun, among his great Museum of Absurdities, looks down upon at present.'

Curious enough: the model of the world just now is England and her Constitution; all Nations striving towards it: poor France swimming these last sixty years in seas of horrid dissolution and confusion, resolute to attain this blessedness of free voting, or to die in chase of it. Prussia too, solid Germany itself, has all broken out into crackling of musketry, loud pamphleteering and Frankfort parliamenting and palavering; Germany too will scale the sacred mountains, how steep soever, and, by talisman of ballot-box, inhabit a political Elysium henceforth. All the Nations have that one hope. Very notable, and rather sad to the humane onlooker. For it is sadly conjectured, all the Nations labour somewhat under a mistake as to England, and the causes of her freedom and her prosperous cotton-spinning; and have much misread the nature of her Parliament, and the effect of ballot-boxes and universal-suffrages there.

What if it were because the English Parliament was from the first, and is only just now ceasing to be, a Council of actual Rulers, real Governing Persons (called Peers, Mitred Abbots, Lords, Knights of the Shire, or howsoever called), actually *ruling* each his section of the country,—and possessing (it must be said) in the lump, or when assembled as a Council, uncommon patience, devoutness, probity, discretion and good fortune,—that the said Parliament ever came to be good for much? In that case it will not be easy to 'imitate' the English Parliament; and the ballot-box and suffrage will be the mere bow of Robin Hood, which it is given to very few to bend, or shoot with to any perfection. And if the Peers become mere big Capitalists, Railway Directors, gigantic Hucksters, Kings of Scrip, *without* lordly quality, or other virtue except cash; and the Mitred Abbots change to mere Able-Editors, masters of Parliamentary Eloquence, Doctors of Political Economy, and suchlike; and all *have* to be elected by a universal-suffrage ballot-box,—I do not see how the English Parliament itself will long continue sea-worthy! Nay, I find England in her own big dumb heart, wherever you come upon her in a silent meditative hour, begins to have dreadful misgivings about it.

The model of the world, then, is at once unattainable by the world, and not much worth attaining? England, as I read the omens, is now called a second time to 'show the Nations how to live;' for by her Parliament, as chief governing entity, I fear she is not long for this world! Poor England must herself again, in these new strange times, the old methods being quite worn out, 'learn how to live.' That now is the terrible problem for England, as for all the Nations; and she alone of all, not *yet* sunk into open Anarchy, but left with time for repentance and amendment; she, wealthiest of all in material resource, in spiritual energy, in ancient loyalty to law, and in the qualities that yield such loyalty,—she perhaps alone of all may be able, with huge travail, and the strain of all her faculties, to accomplish some solution. She will have to try it, she has now to try it; she must accomplish it, or perish from her place in the world!

England, as I persuade myself, still contains in it many *kings*;

The Present Time

possesses, as Old Rome did, many men not needing 'election' to command, but eternally elected for it by the Maker Himself. England's one hope is in these, just now. They are among the silent, I believe; mostly far away from platforms and public palaverings; not speaking forth the image of their nobleness in transitory words, but imprinting it, each on his own little section of the world, in silent facts, in modest valiant actions, that will endure forevermore. They must sit silent no longer. They are summoned to assert themselves; to act forth, and articulately vindicate, in the teeth of howling multitudes, of a world too justly *maddened* into all manner of delirious clamours, what of wisdom they derive from God. England, and the Eternal Voices, summon them; poor England never so needed them as now. Up, be doing everywhere: the hour of crisis has verily come! In all sections of English life, the god-made *king* is needed; is pressingly demanded in most; in some, cannot longer, without peril as of conflagration, be dispensed with. He, wheresoever he finds himself, can say, "Here too am I wanted; here is the kingdom I have to subjugate, and introduce God's Laws into,—God's Laws, instead of Mammon's and M'Croudy's and the Old Anarch's! Here is my work, here or nowhere."——Are there many such, who will answer to the call, in England? It turns on that, whether England, rapidly crumbling in these very years and months, shall go down to the Abyss as her neighbours have all done, or survive to new grander destinies *without* solution of continuity! Probably the chief question of the world at present.

The true 'commander' and king; he who knows for himself the divine Appointments of this Universe, the Eternal Laws ordained by God the Maker, in conforming to which lies victory and felicity, in departing from which lies, and forever must lie, sorrow and defeat, for each and all of the Posterity of Adam in every time and every place; he who has sworn fealty to these, and dare alone against the world assert these, and dare not with the whole world at his back deflect from these;—he, I know too well, is a rare man. Difficult to discover; not quite discoverable, I apprehend, by manoeuvring of ballot-boxes, and riddling of the popular clamour according to the most approved methods. He is not sold at any shop I know of,—though sometimes, as at the sign of the Ballot-box, he is advertised for sale. Difficult indeed to discover: and not very much assisted, or encouraged in late times, to discover *himself*;—which, I think, might be a kind of help? Encouraged rather, and commanded in all ways, if he be wise, to *hide* himself, and give place to the windy Counterfeit of himself; such as the universal-suffrages can recognise, such as loves the most sweet voices of the universal-suffrages!—O Peter, what becomes of such a People; what can become?

Did you never hear, with the mind's ear as well, that fateful Hebrew Prophecy, I think the fatefulest of all, which sounds daily through the streets, "Ou' clo'! Ou' clo'!"—A certain People, once upon a time, clamorously voted by overwhelming majority, "Not *he*; Barabbas, not he! *Him* and what he is, and what he deserves, we know well enough: a reviler of the Chief Priests and sacred Chancery wigs; a seditious Heretic, physical-force Chartist, and enemy of his country and mankind: To the gallows and the cross with him! Barabbas is our man; Barabbas, we are for Barabbas!" They got Barabbas:— have you well considered what a fund of purblind obduracy, of opaque *flunkyism* grown truculent and transcendent; what an eye for the phylacteries, and want of eye for the eternal noblenesses; sordid loyalty to the prosperous Semblances, and high-treason against the Supreme Fact, such a vote betokens in these natures? For it was the consummation of a long series of such; they and their fathers had long kept voting so. A singular People; who could both produce such divine men, and then could so stone and crucify them; a People terrible from the beginning!—Well, they got Barabbas; and they got, of course, such guidance as Barabbas and the like of him could give them; and, of course, they stumbled ever downwards and devilwards, in their truculent stiffnecked way; and—and, at this hour, after eighteen centuries of sad fortune, they prophetically sing "Ou' clo'!" in all the cities of the world. Might the world, at this late hour, but take note of them, and understand their song a little!

Yes, there are some things the universal-suffrage can decide,—and about these it will be exceedingly useful to consult the universal-suffrage: but in regard to most things of importance, and in regard to the choice of men especially, there is (astonishing as it may seem) next to no capability on the part of universal-suffrage.—I request all candid persons, who have never so little originality of mind, and every man has a little, to consider this. If true, it involves such a change in our now-fashionable modes of procedure as fills me with astonishment and alarm. *If* popular suffrage is not the way of ascertaining what the Laws of the Universe are, and who it is that will best guide us in the way of these,—then woe is to us if we do not take another method. Delolme on the British Constitution will not save us; deaf will the Parcæ be to votes of the House, to leading-articles, constitutional philosophies. The other method—alas, it involves a stopping short, or vital change of direction, in the glorious career which all Europe, with shouts heaven-high, is now galloping along: and that, happen when it may, will, to many of us, be probably a rather surprising business!

One thing I do know, and can again assert with great confidence, supported by the whole Universe, and by some Two-hundred generations of men, who have left us some record of themselves there, That the few Wise will have, by one method or another, to take command of the innumerable Foolish; that they must be got to take it;—and that, in fact, since Wisdom, which means also Valour and heroic Nobleness, is alone strong in this world, and one wise man is stronger than all men unwise, they can be got. That they must take it; and having taken, must keep it, and do their God's-Message in it, and defend the same, at their life's peril, against all men and devils. This I do clearly believe to be the backbone of all Future Society, as it has been of all Past; and that without it, there is no Society possible in the world. And what a business *this* will be, before it end in some degree of victory again, and whether the time for shouts of triumph and tremendous cheers upon it is yet come, or not yet by a great way, I perceive too well! A business to make us all very serious indeed. A business not to be accomplished but by noble manhood, and devout all-daring, all-enduring loyalty to Heaven, such as fatally *sleeps* at present,—such as is not *dead* at present either, unless the gods have doomed this world of theirs to die! A business which long centuries of faithful travail and heroic agony, on the part of all the noble that are born to us, will not end; and which to us, of this 'tremendous cheering' century, it were blessedness very great to see successfully begun. Begun, tried by all manner of methods, if there is one wise Statesman or man left among us, it verily must be;—begun, successfully or unsuccessfully, we do hope to see it!

Carlyle

In all European countries, especially in England, one class of Captains and commanders of men, recognisable as the beginning of a new real and not imaginary 'Aristocracy,' has already in some measure developed itself: the Captains of Industry;—happily the class who above all, or at least first of all, are wanted in this time. In the doing of material work, we have already men among us that can command bodies of men. And surely, on the other hand, there is no lack of men needing to be commanded: the sad class of brother-men whom we had to describe as 'Hodge's emancipated horses,' reduced to roving famine,—this too has in all countries developed itself; and, in fatal geometrical progression, is ever more developing itself, with a rapidity which alarms every one. On this ground, if not on all manner of other grounds, it may be truly said, the 'Organisation of Labour' (*not* organisable by the mad methods tried hitherto) is the universal vital Problem of the world.

To bring these hordes of outcast captainless soldiers under due captaincy? This is really the question of questions; on the answer to which turns, among other things, the fate of all Governments, constitutional and other,—the possibility of their continuing to exist, or the impossibility. Captainless, uncommanded, these wretched outcast 'soldiers,' since they cannot starve, must needs become banditti, street-barricaders,—destroyers of every Government that *cannot* put them under captains, and send them upon enterprises, and in short render life human to them. Our English plan of Poor Laws, which we once piqued ourselves upon as sovereign, is evidently fast breaking down. Ireland, now admitted into the Idle Workhouse, is rapidly bursting it in pieces. That never was a 'human' destiny for any honest son of Adam; nowhere but in England could it have lasted at all; and now, with Ireland sharer in it, and the fulness of time come, it is as good as ended. Alas, yes. Here in Connemara, your crazy Ship of the State, otherwise dreadfully rotten in many of its timbers I believe, has sprung a leak: spite of all hands at the pump, the water is rising; the Ship, I perceive, will founder, if you cannot stop this leak!

To bring these Captainless under due captaincy? The anxious thoughts of all men that do think are turned upon that question; and their efforts, though as yet blindly and to no purpose, under the multifarious impediments and obscurations, all point thitherward. Isolated men, and their vague efforts, cannot do it. Government everywhere is called upon,—in England as loudly as elsewhere,—to give the initiative. A new strange task of these new epochs; which no Government, never so 'constitutional,' can escape from undertaking. For it is vitally necessary to the existence of Society itself; it must be undertaken, and succeeded in too, or worse will follow,—and, as we already see in Irish Connaught and some other places, will follow soon. To whatever thing still calls itself by the name of Government, were it never so constitutional and impeded by official impossibilities, all men will naturally look for help, and direction what to do, in this extremity. If help or direction is not given; if the thing called Government merely drift and tumble to and fro, no-whither, on the popular vortexes, like some carcass of a drowned ass, constitutionally put 'at the top of affairs,'—popular indignation will infallibly accumulate upon it; one day, the popular lightning, descending forked and horrible from the black air, will annihilate said supreme carcass, and smite *it* home to its native ooze again!—Your Lordship, this is too true, though irreverently spoken: indeed one knows not how to speak of it; and to me it is infinitely sad and miserable, spoken or not!—Unless perhaps the Voluntary Principle will still help us through? Perhaps this Irish leak, in such a rotten distressed condition of the Ship, with all the crew so anxious about it, will be kind enough to stop of itself?—

Dismiss that hope, your Lordship! Let all real and imaginary Governors of England, at the pass we have arrived at, dismiss forever that fallacious fatal solace to their donothingism: of itself, too clearly, the leak will never stop; by human skill and energy it must be stopped, or there is nothing but the sea-bottom for us all! A Chief Governor of England really ought to recognise his situation; to discern that, doing nothing, and merely drifting to and fro, in however constitutional a manner, he is a squanderer of precious moments, moments that perhaps are priceless; a truly alarming Chief Governor. Surely, to a Chief Governor of England, worthy of that high name,—surely to him, as to every living man, in every conceivable situation short of the Kingdom of the Dead,—there is *something* possible; some plan of action other than that of standing mildly, with crossed arms, till he and we—sink? Complex as his situation is, he, of all Governors now extant among these distracted Nations, has, as I compute, by far the greatest possibilities. The Captains, actual or potential, are there, and the million Captainless: and such resources for bringing them together as no other has. To these outcast soldiers of his, unregimented roving banditti for the present, or unworking workhouse prisoners who are almost uglier than banditti; to these floods of Irish Beggars, Able-bodied Paupers, and nomadic Lackalls, now stagnating or roaming everywhere, drowning the face of the world (too truly) into an untenantable swamp and Stygian quagmire, has the Chief Governor of this country no word whatever to say? Nothing but "Rate in aid," "Time will mend it," "Necessary business of the Session;" and "After me the Deluge"? A Chief Governor that can front his Irish difficulty, and steadily contemplate the horoscope of Irish and British Pauperism, and whitherward it is leading him and us, in this humour, must be a—What shall we call such a Chief Governor? Alas, in spite of old use and wont,—little other than a tolerated Solecism, growing daily more intolerable! He decidedly ought to have some word to say on this matter,—to be incessantly occupied in getting something which he could practically say!—Perhaps to the following, or a much finer effect?

———

Speech of the British Prime-Minister to the floods of Irish and other Beggars, the able-bodied Lackalls, nomadic or stationary, and the general assembly, outdoor and indoor, of the Pauper Populations of these Realms.

"Vagrant Lackalls, foolish most of you, criminal many of you, miserable all; the sight of you fills me with astonishment and despair. What to do with you I know not; long have I been meditating, and it is hard to tell. Here are some three millions of you, as I count: so many of you fallen sheer over into the abysses of open Beggary; and, fearful to think, every new unit that falls is *loading* so much more the chain that drags the others over. On the edge of the precipice hang uncounted millions; increasing, I am told, at the rate of 1200 a-day. They hang there on the giddy edge, poor souls, cramping themselves down, holding-on with all their strength; but falling, falling one after another; and the chain is getting *heavy*, so that ever more fall; and who at last will stand? What to do

The Present Time

with you? The question, What to do with you? especially since the potato died, is like to break my heart!

"One thing, after much meditating, I have at last discovered, and now know for some time back: That you cannot be left to roam abroad in this unguided manner, stumbling over the precipices, and loading ever heavier the fatal *chain* upon those who might be able to stand; that this of locking you up in temporary Idle Workhouses, when you stumble, and subsisting you on Indian meal, till you can sally forth again on fresh roamings, and fresh stumblings, and ultimate descent to the devil;—that this is *not* the plan; and that it never was, or could out of England have been supposed to be, much as I have prided myself upon it!

"Vagrant Lackalls, I at last perceive, all this that has been sung and spoken, for a long while, about enfranchisement, emancipation, freedom, suffrage, civil and religious liberty over the world, is little other than sad temporary jargon, brought upon us by a stern necessity,—but now ordered by a sterner to take itself away again a little. Sad temporary jargon, I say: made-up of sense and nonsense,—sense in small quantities, and nonsense in very large;—and, if taken for the whole or permanent truth of human things, it is no better than fatal infinite nonsense eternally *untrue*. All men, I think, will soon have to quit this, to consider this as a thing pretty well achieved; and to look-out towards another thing much more needing achievement at the time that now is.

"All men will have to quit it, I believe. But to you, my indigent friends, the time for quitting it has palpably arrived! To talk of glorious self-government, of suffrages and hustings, and the fight of freedom and suchlike, is a vain thing in your case. By all human definitions and conceptions of the said fight of freedom, you for your part have lost it, and can fight no more. Glorious self-government is a glory not for you,—not for Hodge's emancipated horses, nor you. No; I say. No. You, for your part, have tried it, and *failed*. Left to walk your own road, the will-o'-wisps beguiled you, your short sight could not descry the pitfalls; the deadly tumult and press has whirled you hither and thither, regardless of your struggles and your shrieks; and here at last you lie; fallen flat into the ditch, drowning there and dying, unless the others that are still standing please to pick you up. The others that still stand have their own difficulties, I can tell you!—But you, by imperfect energy and redundant appetite, by doing too little work and drinking too much beer, you (I bid you observe) have proved that you cannot do it! You lie there plainly in the ditch. And I am to pick you up again, on these mad terms; help you ever again, as with our best heart's-blood, to do what, once for all, the gods have made impossible? To load the fatal chain with your perpetual staggerings and sprawlings; and ever again load it, till we all lie sprawling? My indigent, incompetent friends, I will not! Know that, whoever may be 'sons of freedom,' you for your part are not and cannot be such. Not 'free' you, I think, whoever may be free. You palpably are fallen captive,—*caitiff*, as they once named it:—you do, silently, but eloquently, demand, in the name of mercy itself, that some genuine command be taken of you.

"Yes, my indigent incompetent friends; some genuine practical command. Such,—if I rightly interpret those mad Chartisms, Repeal Agitations, Red Republics, and other delirious inarticulate bowlings and bellowings which all the populations of the world now utter, evidently cries of pain on their and your part,—is the demand which you, Captives, make of all men that are not Captive, but are still Free. Free men,—alas, had you ever any notion who the free men were, who the not-free, the incapable of freedom! The free men, if you could have understood it, they are the wise men; the patient, self-denying, valiant; the Nobles of the World; who can discern the Law of this Universe, what it is, and piously *obey* it; these, in late sad times, having cast you loose, you are fallen captive to greedy sons of profit-and-loss; to bad and ever to worse; and at length to Beer and the Devil. Algiers, Brazil or Dahomey hold nothing in them so authentically *slave* as you are, my indigent incompetent friends!

"Good Heavens, and I have to raise some eight or nine millions annually, six for England itself, and to wreck the morals of my working population beyond all money's worth, to keep the life from going out of *you*: a small service to you, as I many times bitterly repeat! Alas, yes; before high Heaven I must declare it such. I think the old Spartans, who would have killed you instead, had shown more 'humanity,' more of *man*hood, than I thus do! More humanity, I say, more of manhood, and of sense for what the dignity of man demands imperatively of you and of me and of us all. We call it charity, beneficence, and other fine names, this brutish Workhouse

Scheme of ours; and it is but sluggish heartlessness, and insincerity, and cowardly lowness of soul. Not 'humanity' or manhood, I think; perhaps *ape*hood rather,—paltry imitancy, from the teeth outward, of what our heart never felt nor *our* understanding ever saw; dim indolent adherence to extraneous hearsays and extinct traditions; traditions now really about extinct; not living now to almost any of us, and still haunting with their spectralities and gibbering *ghosts* (in a truly baleful manner) almost all of us! Making this our struggling 'Twelfth Hour of the Night' inexpressibly hideous!—

"But as for you, my indigent incompetent friends, I have to repeat with sorrow, but with perfect clearness, what is plainly undeniable, and is even clamorous to get itself admitted, that you are of the nature of *slaves*,—or if you prefer the word, of *nomadic, and now even vagrant and vagabond, servants that can find no master on those terms*; which seems to me a much uglier word. Emancipation? You have been 'emancipated' with a vengeance! Foolish souls, I say the whole world cannot emancipate you. Fealty to ignorant Unruliness, to gluttonous sluggish Improvidence, to the Beer-pot and the Devil, who is there that can emancipate a man in that predicament? Not a whole Reform Bill, a whole French Revolution executed for his behoof alone: nothing but God the Maker can emancipate him, by making him anew.

"To forward which glorious consummation, will it not be well, O indigent friends, that you, fallen flat there, shall henceforth learn to take advice of others as to the methods of standing? Plainly I let you know, and all the world and the worlds know, that I for my part mean it so. Not as glorious unfortunate sons of freedom, but as recognised captives, as unfortunate fallen brothers requiring that I should command you, and if need were, control and compel you, can there henceforth be a relation between us. Ask me not for Indian meal; you shall be compelled to earn it first; know that on other terms I will not give you any. Before Heaven and Earth, and God the Maker of us all, I declare it is a scandal to see *such* a life kept in you, by the sweat and heart's-blood of your brothers; and that, if we cannot mend it, death were preferable! Go to, we must get out of this unutterable coil of nonsenses, constitutional, philanthropical &c., in which (surely without mutual hatred, if with less of 'love' than is supposed) we are all strangling one another!

Carlyle

"Your want of wants, I say, is that you be *commanded* in this world, not being able to command yourselves. Know therefore that it shall be so with you. Nomadism, I give you notice, has ended; needful permanency, soldier-like obedience, and the opportunity and the necessity of hard steady labour for your living, have begun. Know that the Idle Workhouse is shut against you henceforth; you cannot enter there at will, nor leave at will;—you shall enter a quite other Refuge, under conditions strict as soldiering, and not leave till I have done with you. He that prefers the glorious (or perhaps even the rebellious *in*glorious) 'career of freedom,' let him prove that he can travel there, and be the master of himself; and right good speed to him. He who has proved that he cannot travel there or be the master of himself,—let him, in the name of all the gods, become a servant, and accept the just rules of servitude!

"Arise, enlist in my Irish, my Scotch and English 'Regiments of the New Era,'—which I have been concocting, day and night, during these three Grouse-seasons (taking earnest incessant counsel, with all manner of Industrial Notabilities and men of insight, on the matter), and have now brought to a kind of preparation for incipiency, thank Heaven! Enlist there, ye poor wandering banditti; obey, work, suffer, abstain, as all of us have had to do: so shall you be useful in God's creation, so shall you be helped to gain a manful living for yourselves; not otherwise than so. Industrial Regiments"— [*Here numerous persons, with big wigs many of them, and austere aspect, whom I take to be Professors of the Dismal Science, start up in an agitated vehement manner: but the Premier resolutely beckons them down again*]—"Regiments not to fight the French or others, who are peaceable enough towards us; but to fight the Bogs and Wildernesses at home and abroad, and to chain the Devils of the Pit which are walking too openly among us.

"Work, for you? Work, surely, is not quite undiscoverable in an Earth so wide as ours, if we will take the right methods for it! Indigent friends, we will adopt this new relation (which is *old* as the world); this will lead us towards such. Rigorous conditions, not to be violated on either side, lie in this relation; conditions planted there by God Himself; which woe will betide us if we do not discover, gradually more and more discover, and conform to! Industrial Colonels, Workmasters, Taskmasters, Life-commanders, equitable as Rhadamanthus

The Present Time

and inflexible as he; such, I perceive, you do need; and such, you being once put under law as soldiers are, will be discoverable for you. I perceive, with boundless alarm, that I shall have to set about discovering such,—I, since I am at the top of affairs, with all men looking to me. Alas, it is my new task in this New Era; and God knows, I too, little other than a redtape Talking-machine, and unhappy Bag of Parliamentary Eloquence hitherto, am far behind with it! But street-barricades rise everywhere: the hour of Fate has come. In Connemara there has sprung a leak, since the potato died; Connaught, if it were not for Treasury-grants and rates-in-aid, would have to recur to Cannibalism even now, and Human Society would cease to pretend that it existed there. Done this thing must be. Alas, I perceive that if I cannot do it, then surely I shall die, and perhaps shall not have Christian burial! But I already raise near upon Ten Millions for feeding you in idleness, my nomadic friends; work, under due regulations, I really might try to get of"—[*Here arises indescribable uproar, no longer repressible, from all manner of Economists, Emancipationists, Constitutionalists, and miscellaneous Professors of the Dismal Science, pretty numerously scattered about; and cries of "Private Enterprise", "Rights of Capital," "Voluntary Principle," "Doctrines of the British Constitution," swollen by the general assenting hum of all the world, quite drown the Chief Minister for a while. He, with invincible resolution, persists; obtains hearing again:*]

"Respectable Professors of the Dismal Science, soft you a little. Alas, I know what you would say. For my sins, I have read much in those inimitable volumes of yours,—really I should think, some barrowfuls of them in my time,—and, in these last forty years of theory and practice, have pretty well seized what of Divine Message you were sent with to me. Perhaps as small a message, give me leave to say, as ever there was such a noise made about before. Trust me, I have not forgotten it, shall never forget it. Those Laws of the Shop-till are indisputable to me; and practically useful in certain departments of the Universe, as the multiplication-table itself. Once I even tried to sail through the Immensities with them, and to front the big coming Eternities with them; but I found it would not do. As the Supreme Rule of Statesmanship, or Government of Men,—since this Universe is not wholly a Shop,—no. You rejoice in my improved tariffs, free-trade movements and the like, on every hand; for which be thankful, and even sing litanies if you choose. But here at last, in the Idle-Workhouse movement,—unexampled yet on Earth or in the waters under the Earth,—I am fairly brought to a stand; and have had to make reflections, of the most alarming, and indeed awful, and as it were religious nature! Professors of the Dismal Science, I perceive that the length of your tether is now pretty well run; and that I must request you to talk a little lower in future. By the side of the shop-till,—see, your small 'Law of God' is hung up, along with the multiplication-table itself. But beyond and above the shop-till, allow me to say, you shall as good as hold your peace. Respectable Professors, I perceive it is not now the Gigantic Hucksters, but it is the Immortal Gods, yes they, in their terror and their beauty, in their wrath and their beneficence, that are coming into play in the affairs of this world! Soft you a little. Do not you interrupt me, but try to understand and help me!—

—"Work, was I saying? My indigent unguided friends, I should think some work might be discoverable for you. Enlist, stand drill; become, from a nomadic Banditti of Idleness, Soldiers of Industry! I will lead you to the Irish Bogs, to the vacant desolations of Connaught now falling into Cannibalism, to mistilled Connaught, to ditto Munster, Leinster, Ulster, I will lead you: to the English fox-covers, furze-grown Commons, New Forests, Salisbury Plains: likewise to the Scotch Hill-sides, and bare rushy slopes, which as yet feed only sheep, —moist uplands, thousands of square miles in extent, which are destined yet to grow green crops, and fresh butter and milk and beef without limit (wherein no 'Foreigner can compete with us'), were the Glasgow sewers once opened on them, and you with your Colonels carried thither. In the Three Kingdoms, or in the Forty Colonies, depend upon it, you shall be led to your work!

"To each of you I will then say: Here is work for you; strike into it with manlike, soldierlike obedience and heartiness, according to the methods here prescribed,—wages follow for you without difficulty; all manner of just remuneration, and at length emancipation itself follows. Refuse to strike into it; shirk the heavy labour, disobey the rules,—I will admonish and endeavour to incite you; if in vain, I will flog you; if still in vain, I will at last shoot you,—and make God's Earth, and the forlorn-hope in God's Battle, free of you. Understand it,

The Present Time

I advise you! The Organisation of Labour"——[*Left speaking*, says our reporter.]

'Left speaking:' alas, that he should have to 'speak' so much! There are things that should be done, not spoken; that till the doing of them is begun, cannot well be spoken. He may have to 'speak' seven years yet, before a spade be struck into the Bog of Allen; and then perhaps it will be too late!—

You perceive, my friends, we have actually got into the 'New Era' there has been such prophesying of: here we all are, arrived at last;—and it is by no means the land flowing with milk and honey we were led to expect! Very much the reverse. A terrible *new* country this: no neighbours in it yet, that I can see, but irrational flabby monsters (philanthropic and other) of the giant species; hyænas, laughing hyænas, predatory wolves; probably *devils*, blue (or perhaps blue-and-yellow) devils, as St. Guthlac found in Croyland long ago. A huge untrodden haggard country, the 'chaotic battle-field of Frost and Fire;' a country of savage glaciers, granite mountains, of foul jungles, unhewed forests, quaking bogs;—which we shall have our own ados to make arable and habitable, I think! We must stick by it, however;—of all enterprises the impossiblest is that of getting out of *it*, and shifting into another. To work, then, one and all; hands to work!

1st February 1850

THE
MODERN WORKER

I: Phenomena

But, it is said, our religion is gone; we no longer believe in St. Edmund, no longer see the figure of him 'on the rim of the sky,' minatory or confirmatory! God's absolute Laws, sanctioned by an eternal Heaven and an eternal Hell, have become Moral Philosophies, sanctioned by able computations of Profit and Loss, by weak considerations of Pleasures of Virtue and the Moral Sublime.

It is even so. To speak in the ancient dialect, we 'have forgotten God;'—in the most modern dialect and very truth of the matter, we have taken up the Fact of this Universe as it *is not*. We have quietly closed our eyes to the eternal Substance of things, and opened them only to the Shews and Shams of things. We quietly believe this Universe to be intrinsically a great unintelligible Perhaps; extrinsically, clear enough, it is a great, most extensive Cattlefold and workhouse, with most extensive Kitchen-ranges, Dining-tables,—whereat he is wise who can find a place! All the Truth of this Universe is uncertain; only the profit and loss of it, the pudding and praise of it, are and remain very visible to the practical man.

There is no longer any God for us! God's Laws are become a Greatest-Happiness Principle, a Parliamentary Expediency: the Heavens overarch us only as an Astronomical Time-keeper; a butt for Herschel-telescopes to shoot science at, to shoot sentimentalities at:—in our and old Johnson's dialect, man has lost the *soul* out of him; and now, after the due period,—begins to find the want of it! This is verily the plague-spot; centre of the universal Social Gangrene, threatening all modern things with frightful death. To him that will consider it, here is the stem, with its roots and taproot, with its worldwide upas-boughs and accursed poison exudations, under which the world lies writhing in apathy and agony. You touch the focal-centre of all our diseases, of our frightful nosology of diseases, when you lay your hand on this. There is no religion; there is no God; man has lost his soul, and vainly seeks antiseptic salt. Vainly: in killing Kings, in passing Reform Bills, in French Revolutions, Manchester Insurrections, is found no remedy. The foul elephantine leprosy alleviated for an hour, reappears in new force and desperateness next hour.

For actually this is *not* the real fact of the world; the world is not made so, but otherwise!—Truly, any Society setting out from this No-God hypothesis will arrive at a result or two. The *Un*veracities, escorted, each Unveracity of them by its corresponding Misery and Penalty; the Phantasms, and Fatuities, and ten-years Corn-Law Debatings, that shall walk the Earth at noonday,—must needs be numerous! The Universe being intrinsically a Perhaps, being too probably an 'infinite Humbug,' why should any minor Humbug astonish us? It is all according to the order of Nature; and Phantasms riding with huge clatter along the streets, from end to end of our existence, astonish nobody, Enchanted St. Ives Workhouses and Joe-Manton Aristocracies; giant Working Mammonism near strangled in the partridge-nets of giant-looking Idle Dilettantism,—this, in all its branches, in its thousand thousand modes and figures, is a sight familiar to us.

The Popish Religion, we are told, flourishes extremely in these years; and is the most vivacious-looking religion to be met with at present. "*Elle a trois cents ans dans le ventre*" ["she is three-hundred years old in the womb"] counts M. Jouffroy; "*c'est pour quoi je la respecte!*" ["that is why I respect it"]— The old Pope of Rome, finding it laborious to kneel so long while they cart him through the streets to bless the people on *Corpus-Christi* Day, complains of rheumatism; whereupon his Cardinals consult;—construct him, after some study, a stuffed cloaked figure, of iron and wood, with wool or baked hair; and place it in a kneeling posture. Stuffed figure, or rump of a figure; to this stuffed rump he, sitting at his ease on a lower level, joins, by the aid of cloaks and drapery, his living head and outspread hands; the rump with its cloak kneels, the Pope looks, and holds his hands spread; and so the two in concert bless the Roman population on *Corpus-Christi* Day, as well as they can.

I have considered this amphibious Pope, with the wool-and-iron back, with the flesh head and hands; and endeavoured to calculate his horoscope. I reckon him the remarkablest Pontiff that has darkened God's daylight, or painted himself in the human retina, for these several thousand years. Nay, since Chaos first shivered, and 'sneezed,' as the Arabs say, with the first shaft of sunlight shot through it, what stranger product was there of Nature and Art working together? Here is a Supreme Priest who believes God to be—What, in the name of God, *does* he believe God to be?—and discerns that all worship of God is a scenic phantasmagory of wax-candles, organ-blasts, Gregorian Chants, mass-brayings, purple monsignori, wool-and-iron rumps, artistically spread out,—to save the ignorant from worse.

O reader, I say not who are Belial's elect. This poor amphibious Pope too gives loaves to the Poor; has in him more good latent than he is himself aware of. His poor Jesuits, in the late Italian Cholera, were, with a few German Doctors, the only creatures whom dastard terror had not driven mad: they descended fearless into all gulfs and bedlams; watched over the pillow of the dying, with help, with counsel and hope; shone as luminous fixed stars, when all else had gone out in chaotic night: honour to them! This Poor Pope,—who knows what good is in him? In a Time otherwise too prone to forget, he keeps up the mournfulest ghastly memorial of the Highest, Blessedest, which once was; which, in new fit forms, will again partly have to be. Is he not as a perpetual death's-head and cross-bones, with their *Resurgam* ["I shall rise again"], on the grave of a Universal Heroism,—grave of a Christianity? Such Noblenesses, purchased by the world's best heart's-blood, must not be lost; we cannot afford to lose them, in what confusions soever. To all of us the day will come, to a few of us it has already come, when no mortal, with his heart yearning for a 'Divine Humility,' or other 'Highest form of Valour,' will need to look for it in death's heads, but will see it round him in here and there a beautiful living head. Besides, there is in this poor Pope, and his practice of the Scenic Theory of Worship, a frankness which I rather honour. Not half and half, but with undivided heart does *he* set about worshipping by stage machinery; as if there were now, and could again be, in Nature no other. He will ask you, What other? Under this my Gregorian Chant, and beautiful waxlight Phantasmagory, kindly hidden from you is an Abyss, of black Doubt, Scepticism, nay Sansculottic Jacobinism; an Orcus that has no bottom. Think of that. 'Groby Pool *is* thatched with pancakes,'—as Jeannie Deans's Innkeeper defied it to be! The Bottomless of Scepticism, Atheism, Jacobinism, behold, it is thatched over, hidden from your despair, by stage-properties judiciously arranged. This stuffed rump of mine saves not me only from rheumatism, but you also from what other *isms!* In this your Life-pilgrimage No-whither, a fine Squallacci marching-music, and Gregorian Chant, accompanies you, and the hollow Night of Orcus is well hid!

Yes truly, few men that worship by the rotatory Calabash of the Calmucks do it in half so great, frank or effectual a way. Drury-lane, it is said, and that is saying much, might learn from him in the dressing of parts, in the arrangement of lights and shadows. He is the greatest Play-actor that at present draws salary in this world. Poor Pope; and I am told he is fast growing bankrupt too; and will, in a measurable term of years (a great way *within* the 'three hundred') not have a penny to make his pot boil! His old rheumatic back will then get to rest; and himself and his stage-properties sleep well in Chaos for evermore. Or, alas, why go to Rome for Phantasms walking the streets? Phantasms, ghosts, in this midnight hour, hold jubilee, and screech and jabber; and the question rather were, What high Reality anywhere is yet awake? Aristocracy has become Phantasm-Aristocracy, no longer able to *do* its work, not in the least conscious that it has any work longer to do. Unable, totally careless to *do* its work; careful only to clamour for the *wages* of doing its work,—nay for higher, and *palpably* undue wages, and Corn-Laws and *increase* of rents; the old rate of wages not being adequate now! In hydra-wrestle, giant '*Millo*cracy' so called, a real giant, though as yet a blind one and but half-awake, wrestles and wrings in choking nightmare, 'like to be strangled in the partridge-nets of Phantasm-Aristocracy,' as we said, which fancies itself still to be a giant. Wrestles, as under nightmare, till it do awaken; and gasps and struggles thousand-fold, we may say, in a truly painful manner, through all fibres of our English Existence, in these hours and years! Is our poor English Existence wholly becoming a Nightmare; full of mere Phantasms?—

The Champion of England, cased in iron or tin, rides into Westminster Hall, 'being lifted into his saddle with little assistance,' and there asks, If in the four quarters of the world, under the cope of Heaven, is any man or demon that dare question the right of this King? Under the cope of Heaven no man makes intelligible answer,—as several men ought already to have done. Does not this Champion too know the world; that it is a huge Imposture, and bottomless Inanity, thatched over with bright cloth and other ingenious tissues? Him let us leave there, questioning all men and demons.

Him we have left to his destiny; but whom else have we found? From this the highest apex of things, downwards through all strata and breadths, how many fully awakened Realities have we fallen in with: alas, on the contrary, what troops and populations of Phantasms, not God-Veracities but Devil-Falsities, down to the very lowest stratum,—which now, by such superincumbent weight of Unveracities, lies enchanted in St Ives' Workhouses, broad enough, helpless enough! You will walk in no public thoroughfare or remotest byway of English Existence but you will meet a man, an interest of men, that has given up hope in the Everlasting, True, and placed its hope in the Temporary, half or wholly False. The Honourable Member complains unmusically that there is 'devils-dust' in Yorkshire cloth. Yorkshire cloth—why, the very Paper I now write on is made, it seems, partly of plaster-lime well-smoothed, and obstructs my writing! You are lucky if you can find now any good Paper,—any work really *done*; search where you will, from highest Phantasm apex to lowest Enchanted basis.

Consider for example that great Hat seven-feet high, which now perambulates London Streets; which my Friend Sauerteig regarded justly as one of our English notabilities; "the topmost point as yet," said he, "would it were your culminating and returning point, to which English Puffery has been observed to reach!"—the Hatter in the Strand of London, instead of making better felt-hats than another, mounts a huge lath-and-plaster Hat, seven-feet high, upon wheels; sends a man to drive it through the streets; hoping to be saved *thereby*. He has not attempted to *make* better hats, as he was appointed by the Universe to do, and as with this ingenuity of his he could very probably have done; but his whole industry is turned to *persuade* us that he has made such! He too knows that the Quack has become God. Laugh not at him, O Reader; or do not laugh only. He has ceased to be comic; he is fast becoming tragic. To me this all-deafening blast of Puffery, of poor Falsehood grown necessitous, of poor Heart-Atheism fallen now into Enchanted Workhouses, sounds too surely like a Doom's-blast. I have to say to myself in old dialect: "God's blessing is not written on all this; His curse is written on all this!" Unless perhaps the Universe be a chimera;—some old totally deranged eightday clock, dead as brass; which the Maker, if there ever was any Maker, has long ceased to meddle with?—To my friend Sauerteig this poor seven-feet Hat-Manufacturer, as the topstone of English Puffery, was very notable.

Alas, that we natives note him little, that we view him as a thing of course, is the very burden of the misery. We take it for granted, the most rigorous of us, that all men who have made anything are expected and entitled to make the loudest-possible proclamation of it, and call on a discerning public to reward them for it. Every man his own trumpeter; that is, to a really alarming extent, the accepted rule. Make loudest possible proclamation of your Hat: true proclamation if that will do; if that will not do, then false proclamation,—to such extent of falsity as will serve your purpose; as will not seem too false to be credible!—I answer, once for all, that the fact is not so. Nature requires no man to make proclamation of his doings and hat-makings; Nature forbids all men to make such. There is not a man or hat-maker born into the world but feels, or has felt, that he is degrading himself if he speak of his excellencies and prowesses, and supremacy in his craft: his inmost heart says to him, "Leave thy friends to speak of these; if possible, thy enemies to speak of these; but at all events, thy friends!" He feels that he is already a poor braggart; fast hastening to be a falsity and speaker of the Untruth. Nature's Laws, I must repeat, are eternal: her small still voice, speaking from the inmost heart of us, shall not, under terrible penalties, be disregarded. No one man can depart from the truth without damage to himself; no one million of men; no Twenty-seven Millions of men. Shew me a Nation fallen everywhere into this course, so that each expects it, permits it to others and himself, I will shew you a nation travelling with one assent on the broad way. The broad way, however many Banks of England, Cotton-Mills and Duke's Palaces it may have. Not at happy Elysian fields, and everlasting crowns of victory, earned by silent Valour, will this Nation arrive; but at precipices, devouring gulfs, if it pause not. Nature has ap-

The Modern Worker

pointed happy fields, victorious laurel-crowns; but only to the brave and true: *Un*-nature, what we call Chaos, holds nothing in it but vacuities, devouring gulfs. What are Twenty-seven Millions, and their unanimity? Believe them not: the Worlds and the Ages, God and Nature and All Men say otherwise.

'Rhetoric all this?' No, my brother, very singular to say, it is Fact all this. Cocker's Arithmetic is not truer. Forgotten in these days, it is old as the foundations of the Universe, and will endure till the Universe cease. It is forgotten now; and the first mention of it puckers thy sweet countenance into a sneer: but it will be brought to mind again,—unless indeed the Law of Gravitation chance to cease, and men find that they can walk on vacancy. Unanimity of the Twenty-seven Millions will do nothing; walk not thou with them; fly from them as for thy life. Twenty-seven Millions travelling on such courses, with gold jingling in every pocket, with vivats heaven-high, are incessantly advancing, let me again remind thee, towards the *firm-land's end*,—towards the end and extinction of what Faithfulness, Veracity, real Worth, was in their 'way of life.' Their noble ancestors have fashioned for them a 'life-road;'—in how many thousand senses, this! There is not an old wise Proverb on their tongue, an honest Principle articulated in their hearts into utterance, a wise true method of doing and despatching any work or commerce of men, but helps yet to carry them forward. Life is still possible to them, because all is not yet Puffery, Falsity, Mammon-worship and Unnature; because somewhat is yet Faithfulness, Veracity and Valour. With a certain very considerable finite quantity of Unveracity and Phantasm, social life is still possible; not with an infinite quantity! Exceed your certain quantity, the seven-feet Hat, and all things upwards to the very Champion cased in tin, begin to reel and flounder,—in Manchester Insurrections, Chartisms, Sliding-scales; the Law of Gravitation not forgetting to act. You advance incessantly towards the land's end; you are, literally enough, 'consuming the way.' Step after step, Twenty-seven Million unconscious men;—till you are *at* the land's end; till there is not faithfulness enough among you any more: and the next step now is lifted *not* over land, but into air, over ocean-deeps and roaring abysses:— unless perhaps the Law of Gravitation have forgotten to act?

Oh, it is frightful when a whole Nation, as our Fathers used to say, has 'forgotten God;' has remembered only Mammon, and what Mammon leads to! When your self-trumpeting Hat-maker is the emblem of almost all makers, and workers, and men, that make anything,—from soul-overseerships, body-overseerships, epic poems, acts of parliament, to hats and shoe-blacking! Not one false man but does unaccountable mischief: how much, in a generation or two, will Twenty-seven Millions, mostly false, manage to accumulate? The sum of it, visible in every street, market-place, senate-house, circulating library, cathedral, cotton-mill, and union-workhouse, fills one *not* with a comic feeling!

II: Gospel Of Mammonism

READER, even Christian Reader as thy title goes, hast thou any notion of Heaven and Hell? I rather apprehend, not. Often as the words are on our tongue, they have got a fabulous or semi-fabulous character for most of us, and pass on like a kind of transient similitude, like a sound signifying little.

Yet it is well worth while for us to know, once and always, that they are not a similitude, nor a fable nor a semi-fable; that they are an everlasting highest fact! "No Lake of Sicilian or other sulphur burns now anywhere in these ages," sayest thou? Well, and if there did not! Believe that there does not; believe it if thou wilt, nay hold by it as a real increase, a rise to higher stages, to wider horizons and empires. All this has vanished, or has not vanished; believe as thou wilt as to all this. But that an Infinite of Practical Importance, speaking with strict arithmetical exactness, an *Infinite*, has vanished or can vanish from the Life of any Man: this thou shalt not believe! O brother, the Infinite of Terror, of Hope, of Pity, did it not at any moment disclose itself to thee, indubitable, unnameable? Came it never, like the gleam of *preter*-natural eternal Oceans, like the voice of old Eternities, far-sounding through thy heart of hearts? Never? Alas, it was not thy Liberalism then; it was thy Animalism! The Infinite is more sure than any other fact. But only men can discern it; mere building beavers, spinning arachnes, much more the predatory vulturous and vulpine species, do not discern it well!—

'The word Hell' says Sauerteig, 'is still frequently in use among the English People: but I could not without difficulty ascertain what they meant by it. Hell generally signifies the Infinite Terror, the thing a man *is* infinitely afraid of, and shudders and shrinks from, struggling with his whole soul to escape from it. There is a Hell therefore, if you will consider, which accompanies man, in all stages of his history, and religious or other development: but the Hells of men and Peoples differ notably. With Christians it is the infinite terror of being found guilty before the Just Judge. With old Romans, I conjecture, it was the terror not of Pluto, for whom probably they cared little, but of doing unworthily, doing unvirtuously, which was their word for un*man*fully. And now what is it, if you pierce through his Cants, his oft-repeated Hearsays, what he calls his Worships and so forth,—what is it that the modern English soul does, in very truth, dread infinitely, and contemplate with entire despair? What *is* his Hell; after all these reputable, oft-repeated Hearsays, what is it? With hesitation, with astonishment, I pronounce it to be: The terror of "Not succeeding;" of not making money, fame, or some other figure in the world,—chiefly of not making money! Is not that a somewhat singular Hell?'

Yes, O Sauerteig, it is very singular. If we do not 'succeed,' where is the use of us? We had better never have been born. "Tremble intensely," as our friend the Emperor of China says: *there* is the black Bottomless of Terror; what Sauerteig calls the 'Hell of the English!'—But indeed this Hell belongs naturally to the Gospel of Mammonism, which also has its corresponding Heaven. For there *is* one Reality among so many phantasms; about one thing we are entirely in earnest: The making of money. Working Mammonism does divide the world with idle game-preserving Dilettantism:—thank Heaven that there is even a Mammonism, *any*thing we are in earnest about! Idleness is worst, Idleness alone is without hope: work earnestly at anything, you will by degrees learn to work at almost all things. There is endless hope in work, were it even work at making money.

True, it must be owned, we for the present, with our Mammon-Gospel, have come to strange conclusions. We call it a Society; and go about professing openly the totalest separation, isolation. Our life is not a mutual helpfulness; but rather, cloaked under due laws-of-war, named 'fair competition' and so forth, it is a mutual hostility. We have profoundly forgotten everywhere that *Cash-payment* is not the sole relation of human beings; we think, nothing doubting, that *it* absolves and liquidates all engagements of man. "My starving workers?" answers the rich Mill-owner. "Did not I hire them fairly in the market? Did I not pay them, to the last sixpence, the sum covenanted for? What have I to do with them more?"—Verily Mammon-worship is a melancholy creed. When Cain, for his own behoof, had killed Abel, and was questioned, "Where is thy brother?" he too made answer, "Am I my brother's keeper?" Did I not pay my brother *his* wages, the thing he had merited from me?

O sumptuous Merchant-Prince, illustrious game-preserving Duke, is there no way of 'killing' thy brother but Cain's rude way! 'A good man by the very look of him, by his 'very presence with us as a fellow wayfarer in this Life-pilgrimage, *promises* so much:' woe to him if he forget all such promises, if he never know that they were given! To a deadened soul, seared with the brute Idolatry of Sense, to whom going to Hell is equivalent to not making money, all 'promises,' and moral duties, that cannot be pleaded for in Courts of Requests, address themselves in vain. Money he can be ordered to pay, but nothing more. I have not heard in all Past History, and expect not to hear in all Future History, of any Society anywhere under God's Heaven supporting itself on such Philosophy. The Universe is not made so; it is made otherwise than so. The man or nation of men that thinks it is made so, marches forward nothing doubting, step after step; but marches—whither we know! In these last two centuries of Atheistic Government (near two centuries now, since the blessed restoration of his Sacred Majesty, and Defender of the Faith, Charles Second), I reckon that we have pretty well exhausted what of 'firm earth' there was for us to march on;—and are now, very ominously, shuddering, reeling, and let us hope trying to recoil, on the cliff s edge!—For out of this that we call Atheism come so many other *isms* and falsities, each falsity with its misery at its heels!—A SOUL is not like wind (*spiritus*, or breath) contained within a capsule; the ALMIGHTY MAKER is not like a Clockmaker that once, in old immemorial ages, having *made* his Horologe of a Universe, sits ever since and sees it go! Not at all. Hence comes Atheism; come, as we say, many other *isms*; and as the sum of all, comes Valetism, the *reverse* of Heroism; sad root of all woes whatsoever. For indeed, as no man ever saw the above-said wind-element enclosed within its capsule, and finds it at bottom more deniable than conceivable; so too he finds, in spite of Bridge water Bequests, your Clock-maker Almighty an entirely questionable affair, a deniable affair;—and accordingly denies it, and along with it so much else. Alas, one knows not what and how much else! For the faith in an Invisible, Unnameable, God-like, present everywhere in all that we see and work and suffer, is the essence of all faith whatsoever; and that once denied, or still worse, asserted with lips only, and out of bound prayer-books only, what other thing remains believable? That Cant well-ordered is marketable Cant: that Heroism means gas-lighted Histrionism; that seen with 'clear eyes' (as they call Valet-eyes), no man is a Hero, or ever was a Hero, but all men are Valets and Varlets. The accursed practical quintessence of all sorts of Unbelief! For if there be now no Hero, and the Histrio himself begin to be seen into, what hope is there for the seed of Adam here below? We are the doomed everlasting prey of the Quack; who, now in this guise, now in that, is to filch us, to pluck and eat us, by such modes as are convenient for him. For the modes and guises I care little. The Quack once inevitable, let him come swiftly, let him pluck and eat me,—swiftly, that I may at least have done with him; for in his Quack-world I can have no wish to linger. Though he slay me, yet will I *not* trust in him. Though he conquer nations, and have all the Flunkeys of the Universe shouting at his heels, yet will I know well that *he* is an Inanity; that for him and his there is no continuance appointed, save only in Gehenna and the Pool. Alas, the Atheist world, from its utmost summits of Heaven and Westminster Hall, downwards through poor seven-feet Hats and 'Unveracities fallen hungry,' down to the lowest cellars and neglected hunger-dens of it, is very wretched.

One of Dr. Alison's Scotch facts struck us much.[1] A poor Irish Widow, her husband having died in one of the Lanes of Edinburgh, went forth with her three children, bare of all resource, to solicit help from the Charitable Establishments of that City. At this Charitable Establishment and then at that she was refused: referred from one to the other, helped by none;—till she had exhausted them all; till her strength and heart failed her: she sank down in typhus fever; died, and infected her Lane with fever, so that 'seventeen other persons' died of fever there in consequence. The humane Physician asks thereupon, as with a heart too full for speaking, Would it not have been *economy* to help this poor Widow? She took

---

[1] *Observations on the Management of the Poor in Scotland*: By William Pulteney Alison, M.D. (Edinburgh, 1840)

typhus-fever, and killed seventeen of you!—Very curious. The forlorn Irish Widow applies to her fellow-creatures, as if saying, "Behold I am sinking, bare of help: ye must help me! I am your sister, bone of your bone; one God made us; ye must help me!" They answer, "No; impossible: thou art no sister of ours," But she proves her sisterhood; her typhus-fever kills *them*; they actually were her brothers, though denying it! Had human creature ever to go lower for a proof?

For, as indeed was very natural in such case, all government of the Poor by the Rich has long ago been given over to Supply-and-demand, Laissez-faire and such like, and universally declared to be 'impossible.' "You are no sister of ours; what shadow of proof is there? Here are our parchments, our padlocks, proving indisputably our money-safes to be *ours*, and you to have no business with them. Depart! It is impossible!"—Nay, what wouldst thou thyself have us do? cry indignant readers Nothing, my friends,—till you have got a soul for yourselves again. Till then all things are 'impossible.' Till then I cannot even bid you buy, as the old Spartans would have done, two-pence worth of powder and lead, and compendiously shoot to death this poor Irish Widow: even that is 'impossible' for you. Nothing is left but that she prove her sisterhood by dying, and infecting you with typhus. Seventeen of you lying dead will not deny such proof that she *was* flesh of your flesh; and perhaps some of the living may lay it to heart.

'Impossible:' of a certain two-legged animal with feathers it is said, if you draw a distinct chalk-circle round him, he sits, imprisoned, as if girt with the iron ring of Fate; and will die there, though within sight of victuals, or sit in sick misery there, and be fatted to death. The name of this poor two-legged animal is—Goose; and they make of him, when well fattened, *Pâté de foie gras*, much prized by some!

III: Gospel Of Dilettantism

But after all, the Gospel of Dilettantism, producing a Governing Class who do not govern, nor understand in the least that they are bound or expected to govern, is still mournfuler than that of Mammonism. Mammonism, as we said, at least works; this goes idle. Mammonism has seized some portion of the message of Nature to man; and seizing that, and following it, will seize and appropriate more and more of Nature's message: but Dilettantism has missed it wholly. 'Make money:' that will mean withal, 'Do work in order to make money.' But, 'Go gracefully idle in Mayfair,' what does or can that mean? An idle, game-preserving and even corn-lawing Aristocracy, in such an England as ours: has the world, if we take thought of it, ever seen such a phenomenon till very lately? Can it long continue to see such?

Accordingly the impotent, insolent Donothingism in Practice, and Saynothingism in Speech, which we have to witness on that side of our affairs, is altogether amazing. A Corn-Law demonstrating itself openly, for ten years or more, with 'arguments' to make the angels, and some other classes of creatures, weep! For men are not ashamed to rise in Parliament and elsewhere, and speak the things they do *not* think. 'Expediency,' 'Necessities of Party,' &c. &c! It is not known that the Tongue of Man is a sacred organ; that Man himself is definable in Philosophy as an 'Incarnate *Word*;' the Word not there, you have no Man there either, but a Phantasm instead! In this way it is that Absurdities may live long enough,—still walking, and talking for themselves, years and decades after the brains are quite out! How are 'the knaves and dastards' ever to be got 'arrested' at that rate?—

"No man in this fashionable London of yours," friend Sauerteig would say, "speaks a plain word to me. Every man feels bound to be something more than plain; to be pungent withal, witty, ornamental. His poor fraction of sense has to be perked into some epigrammatic shape, that it may prick into me;—perhaps (this is the commonest) to be topsyturvied, left standing on its head, that I may remember it the better! Such grinning inanity is very sad to the soul of man. Human faces should not grin on one like masks; they should look on one like faces! I love honest laughter, as I do sunlight; but not dishonest: most kinds of dancing too; but the St. Vitus kind not at all! A fashionable wit, *ach Himmel* ["O Heaven"], if you ask, Which, he or a Death's head, will be the cheerier company for me? pray send *not* him!"

Insincere Speech, truly, is the prime material of insincere Action. Action hangs, as it were, *dissolved* in Speech, in Thought whereof Speech is the shadow; and precipitates itself therefrom. The kind of Speech in a man betokens the kind of Action you will get from him. Our Speech, in these modern days, has become amazing. Johnson complained, "Nobody speaks in earnest, Sir; there is no serious conversation." To us all serious speech of men, as that of Seventeenth-Century Puritans, Twelfth-Century Catholics, German Poets of this Century, has become jargon, more or less insane. Cromwell was mad and a quack; Anselm, Becket, Goethe, *ditto, ditto*.

Perhaps few narratives in History or Mythology are more significant than that Moslem one, of Moses and the Dwellers by the Dead Sea. A tribe of men dwelt on the shores of that same Asphaltic Lake; and having forgotten, as we are all too prone to do, the inner facts of Nature, and taken up with the falsities and outer semblances of it, were fallen into sad conditions,—verging indeed towards a certain far deeper Lake. Whereupon it pleased kind Heaven to send them the Prophet Moses, with an instructive word of warning out of which might have sprung 'remedial measures' not a few. But no: the men of the Dead Sea discovered, as the valet-species always does in heroes or prophets, no comeliness in Moses; listened with real tedium to Moses, with light grinning, or with splenetic sniffs and sneers, affecting even to yawn; and signified, in short, that they found him a humbug, and even a bore. Such was the candid theory these men of the Asphalt Lake formed to themselves of Moses, That probably he was a humbug, and certainly he was a bore.

Moses withdrew; but Nature and her rigorous veracities

did not withdraw. The men of the Dead Sea, when we next went to visit them, were all 'changed into Apes;'[1] sitting on the trees there, grinning now in the most *un*affected manner; gibbering and chattering very genuine nonsense; finding the whole Universe now a most indisputable Humbug! The Universe has *become* a Humbug to these Apes who thought it one. There they sit and chatter, to this hour: only, I believe, every Sabbath there returns to them a bewildered half-consciousness, half-reminiscence; and they sit, with their wizzened smoke-dried visages, and such an air of supreme tragicality as Apes may; looking out through those blinking smoke-bleared eyes of theirs, into the wonderfulest universal smoky Twilight and undecipherable disordered Dusk of Things; wholly an Uncertainty, Unintelligibility, they and it; and for commentary thereon, here and there an unmusical chatter or mew:—truest, tragicalest Humbug conceivable by the mind of man or ape! They made no use of their souls; and so have lost them. Their worship on the Sabbath now is to roost there, with unmusical screeches, and half-remember that they had souls.

Didst thou never, O Traveller, fall in with parties of this tribe? Meseems they are grown somewhat numerous in our day.

---

[1] Sale's *Koran* (*Introduction*)

IV: Happy

ALL work, even cotton-spinning, is noble; work is alone noble: be that here said and asserted once more. And in like manner, too, all dignity is painful; a life of ease is not for any man, nor for any god. The life of all gods figures itself to us as a Sublime Sadness,—earnestness of Infinite Battle against Infinite Labour. Our highest religion is named the 'Worship of Sorrow.' For the son of man there is no noble crown, well worn, or even ill worn, but is a crown of thorns!—These things, in spoken words, or still better, in felt instincts alive in every heart, were once well known.

Does not the whole wretchedness, the whole *Atheism* as I call it, of man's ways, in these generations, shadow itself for us in that unspeakable Life-philosophy of his: The pretension to be what he calls 'happy?' Every pitifulest whipster that walks within a skin has his head filled with the notion that he is, shall be, or by all human and divine laws ought to be, 'happy.' His wishes, the pitifulest whipster's, are to be fulfilled for him; his days, the pitifulest whipster's, are to flow on in ever-gentle current of enjoyment, impossible even for the gods. The prophets preach to us, Thou shalt be happy; thou shalt love pleasant things, and find them. The people clamour, Why have we not found pleasant things?

We construct our theory of Human Duties, not on any Greatest-Nobleness Principle, never so mistaken; no, but on a Greatest-Happiness Principle. 'The word *Soul* with us, as in some Slavonic dialects, seems to be synonymous with *Stomach*.' We plead and speak, in our Parliaments and elsewhere, not as from the Soul, but from the Stomach;—wherefore, indeed, our pleadings are so slow to profit. We plead not for God's Justice; we are not ashamed to stand clamouring and pleading for our own 'interests,' our own rents and trade-profits; we say, They are the 'interests' of so many; there is such an intense desire in us for them! We demand Free Trade, with much just vociferation and benevolence, That the poorer classes, who are terribly ill-off at present, may have cheaper New-Orleans bacon. Men ask on Free-trade platforms, How can the indomitable spirit of Englishmen be kept up without plenty of bacon? We shall become a ruined Nation!—Surely, my friends, plenty of bacon is good and indispensable: but I doubt, you will never get even bacon by aiming only at that. You are men, not animals of prey, well-used or ill-used! Your Greatest-Happiness Principle seems to me fast becoming a rather unhappy one.—What if we should cease babbling about 'happiness,' and leave *it* resting on its own basis, as it used to do!

A gifted Byron rises in his wrath; and feeling too surely that he for his part is not 'happy,' declares the same in very violent language, as a piece of news that may be interesting. It evidently has surprised him much. One dislikes to see a man and poet reduced to proclaim on the streets such tidings; but on the whole, as matters go, that is not the most dislikable. Byron speaks the *truth* in this matter. Byron's large audience indicates how true it is felt to be.

'Happy,' my brother? First of all, what difference is it whether thou art happy or not! Today becomes Yesterday so fast, all Tomorrows become Yesterdays; and then there is no question whatever of the 'happiness,' but quite another question. Nay, thou hast such a sacred pity left at least for thyself, thy very pains, once gone over into Yesterday, become joys to thee. Besides, thou knowest not what heavenly blessedness and indispensable sanative virtue was in them; thou shalt only know it after many days, when thou art wiser!—A benevolent old Surgeon sat once in our company, with a Patient fallen sick by gourmandising, whom he had just, too briefly in the Patient's judgment, been examining. The foolish Patient still at intervals continued to break in on our discourse, which rather promised to take a philosophic turn: "But I have lost my appetite," said he, objurgatively, with a tone of irritated pathos; "I have no appetite; I can't eat!"—"My dear fellow," answered the Doctor in mildest tone, "it isn't of the slightest consequence;"—and continued his philosophical discoursings with us!

Or does the reader not know the history of that Scottish iron Misanthrope? The inmates of some town-mansion, in those Northern parts, were thrown into the fearfulest alarm by indubitable symptoms of a ghost inhabiting the next house, or perhaps even the partition-wall! Ever at a certain hour, with preternatural gnarring, growling and screeching, which attended as running bass, there began, in a horrid, semi-articulate, unearthly voice, this song: "Once I was hap-hap-happy, but now I'm *mees*-erable! Clack-clack-clack, gnarr-r-r, whuz-z: Once I was hap-hap-happy, but now I'm *mees*-erable!"—Rest, rest, perturbed spirit;—or indeed, as the good old Doctor said: My dear fellow, it isn't of the slightest consequence! But no; the perturbed spirit could not rest; and to the neighbours, fretted, affrighted, or at least insufferably bored by him, it *was* of such consequence that they had to go and examine in his haunted chamber. In his haunted chamber, they find that the perturbed spirit is an unfortunate—Imitator of Byron? No, is an unfortunate rusty Meatjack, gnarring and creaking with rust and work; and this, in Scottish dialect, is *its* Byronian musical Life-philosophy, sung according to ability!

Truly, I think the man who goes about pothering and uproaring for his 'happiness,'—pothering, and were it ballot-boxing, poem-making, or in what way soever fussing and exerting himself,—he is not the man that will help us to 'get our knaves and dastards arrested!' No; he rather is on the way to increase the number,—by at least one unit and his tail! Observe, too, that this is all a modern affair; belongs not to the old heroic times, but to these dastard new times. 'Happiness our being's end and aim,' all that very paltry speculation, is at bottom, if we will count well, not yet two centuries old in the world.

The only happiness a brave man ever troubled himself with asking much about was, happiness enough to get his work done. Not "I can't eat!" but "I can't work!" that was the burden of all wise complaining among men. It is, after all, the one unhappiness of a man. That he cannot work; that he cannot get his destiny as a man fulfilled. Behold, the day is passing swiftly over, our life is passing swiftly over; and the night cometh when no man can work. The night once come, our happiness, our unhappiness,—it is all abolished; vanished, clean gone; a thing that has been: 'not of the slightest consequence' whether we were happy as eupeptic Curtis, as the fattest pig of Epicurus, or unhappy as Job with potsherds, as musical Byron with Giaours and sensibilities of the heart; as the unmusical Meat-jack with hard labour and rust! But our work,—behold that is not abolished, that has not vanished: our work, behold it remains, or the want of it remains;—for endless Times and Eternities, remains; and that is now the sole question with us forevermore! Brief brawling Day, with its noisy phantasms, its poor paper-crowns tinsel-gilt, is gone; and divine everlasting Night with her star-diadems, with her silences and her veracities, is come! What hast thou done, and how? Happiness, unhappiness: all that was but the *wages* thou hadst; thou hast spent all that, in sustaining thyself hitherward; not a coin of it remains with thee, it is all spent, eaten: and now thy work, where is thy work? Swift, out with it, let us see thy work!

Of a truth, if man were not a poor hungry dastard, and even much of a blockhead withal, he would cease criticising his victuals to such extent; and criticise himself rather, what he does with his victuals!

V: The English

AND yet, with all thy theoretic platitudes, what a depth of practical sense in thee, great England! Depth of sense, of justice, and courage; in which, under all emergencies and world-bewilderments, and under this most complex of emergencies we now live in, there is still hope, there is still assurance!

The English are a dumb people. They can do great acts, but not describe them. Like the old Romans and some few others, *their* Epic Poem is written on the earth's surface: England her Mark! It is complained that they have no artists: one Shakspeare indeed; but for Raphael only a Reynolds; for Mozart nothing but a Mr. Bishop; not a picture, not a song. And yet they did produce one Shakspeare: consider how the element of Shakspearean melody does lie imprisoned in their nature; reduced to unfold itself in mere Cotton-mills, Constitutional Governments, and such like;—all the more interesting when it does become visible, as even in such unexpected shapes it succeeds in doing! Goethe spoke of the Horse, how impressive, almost affecting it was that an animal of such qualities should stand obstructed so; its speech nothing but an inarticulate neighing, its handiness mere *hoof*iness, the fingers all constricted, tied together, the finger-nails coagulated into a mere hoof, shod with iron. The more significant, thinks he, are those eye-flashings of the generous noble quadruped; those prancings, curvings of the neck clothed with thunder.

A Dog of Knowledge has free utterance; but the Warhorse is almost mute, very far from free! It is even so. Truly, your freest utterances are not by any means always the best: they are the worst rather; the feeblest, trivialest; their meaning prompt, but small, ephemeral. Commend me to the silent English, to the silent Romans. Nay, the silent Russians too I believe to be worth something: are they not even now drilling, under much obloquy, an immense semi-barbarous half-world from Finland to Kamtschatka, into rule, subordination, civilisation,—really in an old Roman fashion; speaking no word about it; quietly hearing all manner of vituperative Able Editors speak! While your ever-talking, ever-gesticulating French, for example, what are they at this moment drilling?—Nay, of all animals, the freest of utterance, I should judge, is the genus *Simia*: go into the Indian woods, say all Travellers, and look what a brisk, adroit, unresting Ape-population it is!

The spoken Word, the written Poem, is said to be an epitome of the man; how much more the done Work. Whatsoever of morality and of intelligence; what of patience, perseverance, faithfulness, of method, insight, ingenuity, energy; in a word, whatsoever of Strength the man had in him will lie written in the Work he does. To work: why, it is to try himself against Nature, and her everlasting unerring Laws; these will tell a true verdict as to the man. So much of virtue and of faculty did *we* find in him; so much and no more! He had such capacity of harmonising himself with *me* and my unalterable ever-veracious Laws; of coöperating and working as *I* bade him;—and has prospered, and has not prospered, as you see?—Working as great Nature bade him: does not that mean virtue of a kind; nay, of all kinds? Cotton can be spun and sold, Lancashire operatives can be got to spin it, and at length one has the woven webs and sells them, by following Nature's regulations in that matter: by not following Nature's regulations, you have them not. You have them not;—there is no Cotton-web to sell: Nature finds a bill against you; your 'Strength' is not Strength, but Futility! Let faculty be honoured, so far as it is faculty. A man that can succeed in working is to me always a man.

How one loves to see the burly figure of him, this thick-skinned, seemingly opaque, perhaps sulky, almost stupid Man of Practice, pitted against some light adroit Man of Theory, all equipt with clear logic, and able anywhere to give you Why for Wherefore! The adroit Man of Theory, so light of movement, clear of utterance, with his bow full-bent and quiver full of arrow-arguments,—surely he will strike down the game, transfix everywhere the heart of the matter; triumph everywhere, as he proves that he shall and must do? To your astonishment, it turns out oftenest No. The cloudy-browed, thick-soled, opaque Practicality, with no logic-utterance, in silence mainly, with here and there a low grunt or growl, has in him what transcends all logic-utterance: a Congruity with the Unuttered. The Speakable, which lies atop, as a superficial film, or outer skin, is his or is not his: but the Doable, which reaches down to the World's centre, you find him there!

The rugged Brindley has little to say for himself; the rugged Brindley, when difficulties accumulate on him, retires silent, 'generally to his bed;' retires 'sometimes for 'three days together to his bed, that he may be in perfect 'privacy there,' and ascertain in his rough head how the difficulties can be overcome. The ineloquent Brindley, behold he *has* chained seas together; his ships do visibly float over valleys, invisibly through the hearts of mountains; the Mersey and the Thames, the Humber and the Severn have shaken hands: Nature most audibly answers, Yes! The Man of Theory twangs his full-bent bow; Nature's Fact ought to fall stricken, but does not: his logic arrow glances from it as from a scaly dragon, and the obstinate Fact keeps walking its way. How singular! At bottom you will have to grapple closer with the dragon; take it home to you, by real faculty, not by seeming faculty; try whether you are stronger or it is stronger. Close with it, wrestle it: sheer obstinate toughness of muscle; but much more, what we call toughness of heart, which will mean persistance hopeful and even desperate, unsubduable patience, composed candid openness, clearness of mind: all this shall be 'strength' in wrestling your dragon; the whole man's real strength is in this work, we shall get the measure of him here.

Of all the Nations in the world at present the English are the stupidest in speech, the wisest in action. As good as a 'dumb' Nation, I say, who cannot speak, and have never yet spoken,—spite of the Shakspeares and Miltons who shew us what possibilities there are!—O Mr. Bull, I look in that surly face of thine with a mixture of pity and laughter, yet also with wonder and veneration. Thou complainest not, my illustrious friend; and yet I believe the heart of thee is full of sorrow, of unspoken sadness, seriousness,—profound melancholy (as some have said) the basis of thy being. Unconsciously, for thou speakest of nothing, this great Universe is great to thee. Not by levity of floating, but by stubborn force of swimming, shalt thou make thy way. The Fates sing of thee that thou shalt many times be thought an ass and a dull ox, and shalt with a godlike indifference believe it. My friend,—and it is all untrue, nothing ever falser in point of fact! Thou art of those great ones whose greatness the small passer-by does not discern. Thy very stupidity is wiser than their wisdom. A grand *vis inertiæ* ["force of inertia"] is in thee; how many grand qualities unknown to small men! Nature alone knows thee, acknowledges the bulk and strength of thee: thy Epic, unsung in words, is written in huge characters on the face of this Planet,—sea-moles, cotton-trades, railways, fleets and cities, Indian Empires, Americas, New-Hollands; legible throughout the Solar System!

But the dumb Russians too, as I said, they, drilling all wild Asia and wild Europe into military rank and file, a terrible yet hitherto a prospering enterprise, are still dumber. The old Romans also could not *speak*, for many centuries:—not till the world was theirs; and so many speaking Greekdoms, their logic-arrows all spent, had been absorbed and abolished. The logic-arrows, how they glanced futile from obdurate thick-skinned Facts; Facts to be wrestled down only by the real vigour of Roman thews!—As for me, I honour, in these loud-babbling days, all the Silent rather. A grand Silence that of Romans;—nay the grandest of all, is it not that of the gods! Even Triviality, Imbecility, that can sit silent, how respectable is it in comparison! The 'talent of silence' is our fundamental one. Great honour to him whose Epic is a melodious hexameter Iliad; not a jingling Sham-Iliad, nothing true in it but the hexameters and forms merely. But still greater honour, if his Epic be a mighty Empire slowly built together, a mighty Series of Heroic deeds,—a mighty Conquest over Chaos; *which* Epic the 'Eternal Melodies' have, and must have, informed and dwelt in, as *it* sung itself! There is no mistaking that latter Epic. Deeds are greater than Words. Deeds have such a life, mute bat undeniable, and grow as living trees and fruit-trees do; they people the vacuity of Time, and make it green and worthy. Why should the oak prove logically that it ought to grow, and will grow? Plant it, try it; what gifts of diligent judicious assimilation and secretion it has, of progress and resistance, of *force* to grow, will then declare themselves. My much-honoured, illustrious, extremely inarticulate Mr. Bull!—

Ask Bull his spoken opinion of any matter,—oftentimes the force of dulness can no farther go. You stand silent, incred-

The Modern Worker

ulous, as over a platitude that borders on the Infinite. The man's Churchisms, Dissenterisms, Puseyisms, Benthamisms, College Philosophies, Fashionable Literatures, are unexampled in this world. Fate's prophecy is fulfilled; you call the man an ox and an ass. But set him once to work,—respectable man! His spoken sense is next to nothing, nine-tenths of it palpable *non*sense: but his unspoken sense, his inner silent feeling of what is true, what does agree with fact, what is doable and what is not doable,—this seeks its fellow in the world. A terrible worker; irresistible against marshes, mountains, impediments, disorder, incivilisation; everywhere vanquishing disorder, leaving it behind him as method and order. He 'retires to his bed three days' and considers!

Nay withal, stupid as he is, our dear John,—ever, after infinite tumblings, and spoken platitudes innumerable from barrel-heads and parliament-benches, he does settle down somewhere about the just conclusion; you are certain that his jumblings and tumblings will end, after years or centuries, in the stable equilibrium. Stable equilibrium, I say; centre-of-gravity lowest;—not the unstable, with centre-of-gravity highest, as I have known it done by quicker people! For indeed, do but jumble and tumble sufficiently, you avoid that worst fault, of settling with your centre-of-gravity highest; your centre-of-gravity is certain to come lowest, and to stay there. If slowness, what we in our impatience call 'stupidity,' be the price of stable equilibrium over unstable, shall we grudge a little slowness? Not the least admirable quality of Bull is, after all, that of remaining insensible to logic; holding out for considerable periods, ten years or more, as in this of the Corn-Laws, after all arguments and shadow of arguments have faded away from him, till the very urchins on the street titter at the arguments he brings. Logic,—Λογική, the 'Art of Speech,'—does indeed speak so and so; clear enough: nevertheless Bull still shakes his head; will see whether nothing else *illogical*, not yet 'spoken,' not yet able to be 'spoken,' do not lie in the business, as there so often does!—My firm belief is, that, finding himself now enchanted, hand-shackled, foot-shackled, in Poor-Law Bastilles and elsewhere, he will retire three days to his bed, and *arrive* at a conclusion or two! His three years 'total stagnation of trade,' alas, is not that a painful enough 'lying in bed to consider himself?' Poor Bull!

Bull is a born Conservative; for this too I inexpressibly honour him. All great Peoples are conservatives; slow to believe in novelties; patient of much error in actualities; deeply and forever certain of the greatness that is in Law, in Custom once solemnly established, and now long recognised as just and final.—True, O Radical Reformer, there is no Custom that can, properly speaking, be final; none. And yet thou seest *Customs* which, in all civilised countries, are accounted final; nay, under the Old-Roman name of *Mores*, are accounted *Morality*, Virtue, Laws of God Himself. Such, I assure thee, not a few of them are; such almost all of them once were. And greatly do I respect the solid character,—a block-head, thou wilt say; yes, but a well-conditioned blockhead, and the best-conditioned,—who esteems all 'Customs once solemnly acknowledged' to be ultimate, divine, and the rule for a man to walk by, nothing doubting, not inquiring farther. What a time of it had we, were all men's life and trade still, in all parts of it, a problem, a hypothetic seeking, to be settled by painful Logics and Baconian Inductions! The Clerk in Eastcheap cannot spend the day in verifying his Ready-Reckoner; he must take it as verified, true and indisputable; or his Book-keeping by Double Entry will stand still. "Where is your Posted Ledger?" asks the Master at night.—"Sir," answers the other, "I was verifying my Ready-Reckoner, and find some errors. The Ledger is—!"—Fancy such a thing!

True, all turns on your Ready-Reckoner being moderately correct,—being *not* insupportably incorrect! A Ready-Reckoner which has led to distinct entries in your Ledger such as these: '*Creditor* an English People by fifteen hundred years of good Labour; and *Debtor* to lodging in enchanted Poor-Law Bastilles: *Creditor* by conquering the largest Empire the Sun ever saw; and *Debtor* to Donothingism and "Impossible" written on all departments of the government thereof: *Creditor* by mountains of gold ingots earned; and *Debtor* to No Bread purchasable by them:' *such* Ready-Reckoner, methinks, is beginning to be suspect; nay is ceasing, and has ceased, to be suspect! Such Ready-Reckoner is a Solecism in Eastcheap; and must, whatever be the press of business, and will and shall be rectified a little. Business can go on no longer with *it*. The most Conservative English People, thickest-smkinned, most patient of Peoples, is driven alike by its Logic and its Unlogic, by things 'spoken,' and by things not yet spoken or very speakable, but only felt and very unendurable, to be wholly a Reforming People. Their Life as it is has ceased to be longer possible for them.

Urge not this noble silent People; rouse not the Berserkir-rage that lies in them! Do you know their Cromwells, Hampdens, their Pyms and Bradshaws? Men very peaceable, but men that can be made very terrible! Men who, like their old Teutsch Fathers in Agrippa's days, 'have a soul that despises death;' to whom 'death,' compared with falsehoods and injustices, is light;—'in whom there is a rage unconquerable by the immortal gods!' Before this, the English People have taken very preternatural-looking Spectres by the beard; saying virtually: "And if thou *wert* 'preternatural?' Thou with thy 'divine-rights' grown diabolical wrongs? Thou—not even 'natural;' decapitable; totally extinguishable!"——Yes, just so godlike as this People's patience was, even so godlike will and must its impatience be. Away, ye scandalous Practical Solecisms, children actually of the Prince of Darkness; ye have near broken our hearts; we can and will endure you no longer. Begone, we say; depart while the play is good! By the Most High God, whose sons and born missionaries true men are, ye shall not continue here! You and we have become incompatible; can inhabit one house no longer. Either you must go, or we. Are ye ambitious to try *which* it shall be?

O my Conservative friends, who still specially name and struggle to approve yourselves 'Conservative,' would to Heaven I could persuade you of this world-old fact, than which Fate is not surer, That Truth and Justice alone are *capable* of being 'conserved' and preserved! The thing which is unjust, which is *not* according to God's Law, will you, in a God's Universe, try to conserve that? It is so old, say you? Yes, and the hotter haste ought *you*, of all others, to be in to let it grow no older! If but the faintest whisper in your hearts intimate to you that it is not fair,—hasten, for the sake of Conservatism itself, to probe it rigorously, to cast it forth at once and forever if guilty. How will or can you preserve *it*, the thing that is not fair? 'Impossibility' a thousandfold is marked on that. And ye call yourselves Conservatives, Aristocracies:—ought not honour and nobleness of mind, if they had departed from all the Earth elsewhere, to find their last refuge with you? Ye unfortunate!

The bough that is dead shall be cut away, for the sake of the tree itself. Old? Yes, it is too old. Many a weary winter has it swung and creaked there, and gnawed and fretted, with its dead wood, the organic substance and still living fibre of this good tree; many a long summer has its ugly naked brown defaced the fair green umbrage; every day it has done mischief, and that only: off with it, for the tree's sake, if for nothing more: let the Conservatism that would preserve cut *it* away. Did no wood-forester apprise you that a dead bough with its dead root left sticking there is extraneous, poisonous; is as a dead iron spike, some horrid rusty ploughshare driven into the living substance;—nay is far worse; for in every windstorm ('commercial crisis' or the like), it frets and creaks, jolts itself to and fro, and cannot lie quiet as your dead iron spike would!

If I were the Conservative Party of England (which is another bold figure of speech), I would not for a hundred thousand pounds an hour allow those Corn-Laws to continue. Potosi and Golconda put together would not purchase my assent to them. Do you count what treasuries of bitter indignation they are laying up for you in every just English heart? Do you know what questions, not as to Corn-prices and Sliding-scales alone, they are *forcing* every reflective Englishman to ask himself? Questions insoluble, or hitherto unsolved; deeper than any of our Logic plummets hitherto will sound: questions deep enough,—which it were better that we did not name even in thought! You are forcing us to think of them, to begin uttering them. The utterance of them is begun; and where will it be ended, think you? When two millions of one's brother-men sit in Workhouses, and five millions, as is insolently said, 'rejoice in potatoes,' there are various things that must be begun, let them end where they can.

VI: Two Centuries

THE Settlement effected by our 'Healing Parliament' in the Year of Grace 1660, though accomplished under universal acclamations from the four corners of the British Dominions, turns out to have been one of the mournfulest that ever took place in this land of ours. It called and thought itself a Settlement of the brightest hope and fulfilment, bright as the blaze of universal tar-barrels and bonfires could make it: and we find it now, on looking back on it with the insight which trial has yielded, a Settlement as of despair. Considered well, it was a settlement to govern henceforth without God, with only some decent Pretence of God.

Governing by the Christian Law of God had been found a thing of battle, convulsion, confusion, an infinitely difficult thing: wherefore let us now abandon it, and govern only by so much of God's Christian Law as—as may prove quiet and convenient for us. What is the end of Government? To guide men in the way wherein they should go; towards their true good in this life, the portal of infinite good in a life to come? To guide men in such way, and ourselves in such way, as, the Maker of men, whose eye is upon us, will sanction at the Great Day?—Or alas, perhaps at bottom is there no Great Day, no sure outlook of any life to come; but only this poor life, and what of taxes, felicities, Nell-Gwyns and entertainments we can manage to muster here? In that case, the end of Government will be, To suppress all noise and disturbance, whether of Puritan preaching, Cameronian psalm-singing, thieves'-riot, murder, arson, or what noise soever, and—be careful that supplies do not fail! A very notable conclusion, if we will think of it; and not without an abundance of fruits for us. Oliver Cromwell's body hung on the Tyburn-gallows, as the type of Puritanism found futile, inexecutable, execrable,—yes, that gallows-tree has been a finger-post into very strange country indeed. Let earnest Puritanism die; let decent Formalism, whatsoever cant it be or grow to, live! We have had a pleasant journey in that direction; and are—arriving at our inn?

To support the Four Pleas of the Crown, and keep Taxes coming in: in very sad seriousness, has not this been, ever since, even in the best times, almost the one admitted end and aim of Government? Religion, Christian Church, Moral Duty; the fact that man had a soul at all; that in man's life there was any eternal truth or justice at all,—has been as good as left quietly out of sight. Church indeed,—alas, the endless talk and struggle we have had of High-Church, Low-Church, Church-Extension, Church-in-Danger: we invite the Christian reader to think whether it has not been a too miserable screech-owl phantasm of talk and struggle, as for a 'Church,' which one had rather not define at present!

But now in these godless two centuries, looking at England and her efforts and doings, if we ask, What of England's doings the Law of Nature had accepted, Nature's King had actually furthered and pronounced to have truth in them,— where is our answer? Neither the 'Church' of Hurd and Warburton, nor the Anti-church of Hume and Paine; not in any shape the Spiritualism of England: all this is already seen, or beginning to be seen, for what it is; a thing that Nature does *not* own. On the one side is dreary Cant, with a *reminiscence* of things noble and divine; on the other is but acrid Candour, with a *prophecy* of things brutal, infernal. Hurd and Warburton are sunk into the sere and yellow leaf; no considerable body of true-seeing men looks thitherward for healing: the Paine-and-Hume Atheistic theory of 'things well let alone' with Liberty, Equality and the like, is also in these days declaring itself naught, unable to keep the world from taking fire.

The theories and speculations of both these parties, and we may say, of all intermediate parties and persons, prove to be things which the Eternal Veracity did not accept; things superficial, ephemeral, which already a near Posterity, finding them already dead and brown-leafed, is about to suppress and forget. The Spiritualism of England, for those godless years, is, as it were, all forgettable. Much has been written: but the perennial Scriptures of Mankind have had small accession: from all English Books, in rhyme or prose, in leather binding

The Modern Worker

or in paper wrappage, how many verses have been added to these? Our most melodious Singers have sung as from the throat outwards: from the inner Heart of Man, from the great Heart of Nature, through no Pope or Philips, has there come any tone. The Oracles have been dumb. In brief, the Spoken Word of England has not been true. The Spoken Word of England turns out to have been trivial; of short endurance; not valuable, not available as a Word, except for the passing day. It has been accordant with transitory Semblance; discordant with eternal Fact. It has been unfortunately not a Word, but a Cant; a helpless involuntary Cant, nay too often a cunning voluntary one: either way, a very mournful Cant; the Voice not of Nature and Fact, but of something other than these.

With all its miserable shortcomings, with its wars, controversies, with its trades-unions, famine-insurrections,—it is her Practical Material Work alone that England has to shew for herself! This, and hitherto almost nothing more; yet actually this. The grim inarticulate veracity of the English People, unable to speak its meaning in words, has turned itself silently on things; and the dark powers of Material Nature have answered, "Yes, this at least is true, this is not false!" So answers Nature. "Waste desert-shrubs of the Tropical swamps have become Cotton-trees; and here, under my furtherance, are verily woven shirts,—hanging unsold, undistributed, but capable to be distributed, capable to cover the bare backs of my children of men. Mountains, old as the Creation, I have permitted to be bored through: bituminous fuel-stores, the wreck of forests that were green a million years ago,—I have opened them from my secret rock-chambers, and they are yours, ye English. Your huge fleets, steamships, do sail the sea: huge Indias do obey you; from huge *New* Englands and Antipodal Australias, comes profit and traffic to this Old England of mine!" So answers Nature. The Practical Labour of England is *not* a chimerical Triviality: it is a Fact, acknowledged by all the Worlds; which no man and no demon will contradict. It is, very audibly, though very inarticulately as yet, the one God's Voice we have heard in these two atheistic centuries.

And now to observe with what bewildering obscurations and impediments all this as yet stands entangled, and is yet intelligible to no man! How, with our gross Atheism, we hear it not to be the Voice of God to us, but regard it merely as a Voice of earthly Profit-and-Loss. And have a Hell in England,—the Hell of not making money. And coldly see the all-conquering valiant Sons of Toil sit enchanted, by the million, in their Poor-Law Bastille, as if this were Nature's Law;—mumbling to ourselves some vague janglement of Laissez-faire, Supply-and-demand, Cash-payment the one nexus of man to man: Free-trade, Competition, and Devil take the hindmost, our latest Gospel yet preached!

As if, in truth, there were no God of Labour; as if godlike Labour and brutal Mammonism were convertible terms. A serious, most earnest Mammonism grown Midas-eared; an unserious Dilettantism, earnest about nothing, grinning with inarticulate incredulous incredible jargon about all things, as the *enchanted* Dilettanti do by the Dead Sea! It is mournful enough, for the present hour; were there, not an endless hope in it withal. Giant LABOUR, truest emblem there is of God the World-Worker, Demiurgus, and Eternal Maker; noble Labour, which is yet to be the King of this Earth, and sit on the highest throne,—staggering hitherto like a blind irrational giant, hardly allowed to have his common place on the street-pavements; idle Dilettantism, Dead-Sea Apism, crying out, "Down with him, he is dangerous!"

Labour must become a seeing rational giant, with a *soul* in the body of him, and take his place on the throne of things,—leaving his Mammonism, and several other adjuncts, on the lower steps of said throne.

VII: Over-Production

But what will reflective readers say of a Governing Class, such as ours, addressing its Workers with an indictment of 'Over-production!' Over-production: runs it not so? "Ye miscellaneous, ignoble manufacturing individuals, ye have produced too much! We accuse you of making above two-hundred thousand shirts for the bare backs of mankind. Your trousers, too, which you have made, of fustian, of cassimere, of Scotch-plaid, of jane, nankeen and woollen broad-cloth, are they not manifold? Of hats for the human head, of shoes for the human foot, of stools to sit on, spoons to eat with— Nay, what say we hats or shoes? You produce gold watches, jewelleries, silver forks and epergnes, commodes, chiffoniers, stuffed sofas—Heavens, the Commercial Bazaar and multitudinous Howel-and-Jameses cannot contain you. You have produced, produced;—he that seeks your indictment let him look around. Millions of shirts, and empty pairs of breeches, hang there in judgment against you. We accuse you of over-producing: you are criminally guilty of producing shirts, breeches, hats, shoes and commodities, in a frightful over-abundance. And now there is a glut, and your operatives cannot be fed!"

Never, surely, against an earnest Working Mammonism was there brought, by Game-preserving aristocratic Dilettantism, a stranger accusation, since this world began. My lords and gentlemen,—why, it was *you* that were appointed, by the fact and by the theory of your position on the Earth, to 'make and administer Laws,' that is to say, in a world such as ours, to guard against 'gluts;' against honest operatives, who had done their work, remaining unfed! I say, *you* were appointed to preside over the Distribution and Apportionment of the Wages of Work done; and to see well that there went no labourer without his hire, were it of money-coins, were it of hemp gallows-ropes: that function was yours, and from immemorial time has been; yours, and as yet no other's. These poor shirt-spinners have forgotten much, which by the virtual unwritten law of their position they should have remembered: but by any written recognised law of their position, what have they forgotten? They were set to make shirts. The Community with all its voices commanded them, saying, "Make shirts;"—and there the shirts are! Too many shirts? Well, that is a novelty, in this intemperate Earth, with its nine-hundred millions of bare backs! But the Community commanded you, saying, "See that the shirts are well apportioned, that our Human Laws be emblem of God's Laws;"—and where is the apportionment? Two million shirtless or ill-shirted workers sit enchanted in Workhouse Bastilles, five million more (according to some) in Ugolino Hunger-cellars; and for remedy, you say,—what say you?—Raise *our* rents!" I have not in my time heard any stranger speech, not even on the Shores of the Dead Sea. You continue addressing these poor shirt-spinners and over-producers, in really a *too* triumphant a manner:

"Will you bandy accusations, will you accuse *us* of over-production? We take the Heavens and the Earth to witness that we have produced nothing at all. Not from us proceeds this frightful overplus of shirts. In the wide domains of created Nature, circulates no shirt or thing of our producing. Certain fox-brushes nailed upon our stable-door, the fruit of fair audacity at Melton Mowbray; these we have produced, and they are openly nailed up there. He that accuses us of producing, let him shew himself, let him name what and when. We are innocent of producing;—ye ungrateful, what mountains of things have we not, on the contrary, had to 'consume,' and make away with! Mountains of those your heaped manufacturers, wheresoever edible or wearable, have they not disappeared before us, as if we had the talent of ostriches, of cormorants, and a kind of divine faculty to eat? Ye ungrateful!—and did you not grow under the shadow of our wings? Are not your filthy mills built on these fields of ours; on this soil of England, which belongs to—whom think you? And we shall not offer you our own wheat at the price that pleases us, but that partly pleases you? A precious notion! What would become of you, if we chose, at any time, to decide on growing no wheat more?"

Yes, truly, *here* is the ultimate rock-basis of all Corn-Laws;

whereon, at the bottom of much arguing, they rest, as securely as they can: What would become of you, if we decided, some day, on growing no more wheat at all? If we chose to grow only partridges henceforth, and a modicum of wheat for our own uses? Cannot we do what we like with our own?—Yes, indeed! For my share, if I could melt Gneiss Rock, and create Law of Gravitation; if I could stride out to the Doggerbank, some morning, and striking down my trident there into the mud-waves, say, "Be land, be fields, meadows, mountains, and fresh-rolling streams!" by Heaven, I should incline to have the letting of *that* land in perpetuity, and sell the wheat of it, or burn the wheat of it, according to my own good judgment! My Corn-Lawing friends, you affright me.

To the 'Millo-cracy' so-called, to the Working Aristocracy, steeped too deep in mere ignoble Mammonism, and as yet all unconscious of its noble destinies, as yet but an irrational or semi-rational giant, struggling to awake some soul in itself,— the world will have much to say, reproachfully, reprovingly, admonishingly. But to the Idle Aristocracy, what will the world have to say? Things painful and not pleasant!

To the man who *works*, who attempts, in never so ungracious barbarous a way, to get forward with some work, you will hasten out with furtherances, with encouragements, corrections; you will say to him: "Welcome; thou art ours; our care shall be of thee." To the Idler, again, never so gracefully going idle, coming forward with never so many parchments, you will not hasten out; you will sit still, and be disinclined to rise. You will say to him: "Not welcome, O complex Anomaly; would thou hadst stayed out of doors: for who of mortals knows what to do with thee? Thy parchments: yes, they are old, of venerable yellowness; and we too honour parchment, old-established settlements, and venerable use and wont. Old parchments in very truth:—yet on the whole, if thou wilt remark, they are young to the Granite Rocks, to the Groundplan of God's Universe! We advise thee to put up thy parchments; to go home to thy place, and make no needless noise whatever. Our heart's wish is to save thee: yet there as thou art, hapless Anomaly, with nothing but thy yellow parchments, noisy futilities, and shotbelts and fox-brushes, who of gods or men can avert dark Fate? Be counselled, ascertain if no work exist for thee on God's Earth; if thou find no commanded-duty there but that of going gracefully idle? Ask, inquire earnestly, with a half-frantic earnestness; for the answer means Existence or Annihilation to thee. We apprise thee of the world-old fact, becoming sternly disclosed again in these days, That he who cannot work in this Universe cannot get existed in it: had he parchments to thatch the face of the world, these, combustible fallible sheep-skin, cannot avail him. Home, thou unfortunate; and let us have at least no noise from thee!"

Suppose the unfortunate Idle Aristocracy, as the unfortunate Working one has done, were to 'retire three days to *its* bed,' and consider itself there, what o'clock it had become?—

How have we to regret not only that men have 'no religion,' but that they have next to no reflection; and go about with heads full of mere extraneous noises, with eyes wide-open but visionless,—for most part, in the somnambulist state!

VIII: Unworking Aristocracy

It is well said, 'Land is the right basis of an Aristocracy;' whoever possesses the Land, he, more emphatically than any other, is the Governor, Viceking of the people on the Land. It is in these days as it was in those of Henry Plantagenet and Abbot Samson; as it will in all days be. The Land is *Mother* of us all; nourishes, shelters, gladdens, lovingly enriches us all; in how many ways, from our first wakening to our last sleep on her blessed mother-bosom, does she, as with blessed mother-arms, enfold us all!

The Hill I first saw the Sun rise over, when the Sun and I and all things were yet in their auroral hour, who can divorce me from it? Mystic, deep as the world's centre, are the roots I have struck into my Native Soil; no *tree* that grows is rooted so. From noblest Patriotism to humblest industrial Mechanism; from highest dying for your country, to lowest quarrying and coal-boring for it, a Nation's Life depends upon its Land. Again and again we have to say, there can be no true Aristocracy but must possess the Land.

Men talk of 'selling' Land. Land, it is true, like Epic Poems and even higher things, in such a trading world, has to be presented in the market for what it will bring, and as we say be 'sold:' but the notion of 'selling,' for certain bits of metal, the *Iliad* of Homer, how much more the *Land* of the World-Creator, is a ridiculous impossibility! We buy what is saleable of it; nothing more was ever buyable. Who can, or could, sell it to us? Properly speaking, the Land belongs to these two: To the Almighty God; and to all His Children of Men that have ever worked well on it, or that shall ever work well on it. No generation of men can or could, with never such solemnity and effort, sell Land on any other principle: it is not the property of any generation, we say, but that of all the past generations that have worked on it, and of all the future ones that shall work on it.

Again, we hear it said, The soil of England, or of any country, is properly worth nothing, except 'the labour bestowed on it.' This, speaking even in the language of Eastcheap, is not correct. The rudest space of country equal in extent to England, could a whole English Nation, with all their habitudes, arrangements, skills, with whatsoever they do carry within the skins of them, and cannot be stript of, suddenly take wing, and alight on it,—would be worth a very considerable thing! Swiftly, within year and day, this English Nation, with its multiplex talents of ploughing, spinning, hammering, mining, road-making and trafficking, would bring a handsome value out of such a space of country. On the other hand, fancy what an English Nation, once 'on the wing,' could have done with itself, had there been simply no soil, not even an inarable one, to alight on? Vain all its talents for ploughing, hammering, and whatever else; there is no Earth-room for this Nation with its talents: this Nation will have to *keep* hovering on the wing, dolefully shrieking to and fro; and perish piecemeal; burying itself, down to the last soul of it, in the waste unfirmamented seas. Ah yes, soil, with or without ploughing, is the gift of God. The soil of all countries belongs evermore, in a very considerable degree, to the Almighty Maker! The last stroke of labour bestowed on it is not the making of its value, but only the increasing thereof.

It is very strange, the degree to which these truisms are forgotten in our days; how, in the ever-whirling chaos of Formulas, we have quietly lost sight of Fact,—which it is so perilous not to keep for ever in sight. Fact, if we do not see it, will make us *feel* it by and by!—From much loud controversy and Corn-Law debating there rises, loud though inarticulate, once more in these years, this very question among others, Who made the Land of England? Who made it, this respectable English Land, wheat-growing, metalliferous, carboniferous, which will let readily hand over head for seventy millions or upwards, as it here lies: who did make it?—"We!" answer the much-*consuming* Aristocracy; "We!" as they ride in, moist with the sweat of Melton Mowbray: "It is we that made it; or are the heirs, assigns and representatives of those who did!"—My brothers, You? Everlasting honor to you, then; and Corn-Laws as many as you will, till your own deep stomachs cry Enough, or some voice of human pity for our famine bids you

Hold! Ye are as gods, that can create soil. Soil-creating gods there is no withstanding. They have the might to sell wheat at what price they list; and the right, to all lengths, and famine-lengths,—if they be pitiless infernal gods! Celestial gods, I think, would stop short of the famine-price; but no infernal nor any kind of god can be bidden stop!——Infatuated mortals, into what questions are you driving every thinking man in England!

I say, you did *not* make the Land of England; and, by the possession of it, you *are* bound to furnish guidance and governance to England! That is the law of your position on this God's-Earth; an everlasting act of Heaven's Parliament, not repealable in St. Stephen's or elsewhere! True government and guidance; not no-government and Laissez-faire; how much less, *mis*government and Corn-Law! There is not an imprisoned Worker looking out from these Bastilles but appeals, very audibly in Heaven's High Courts, against you, and me, and every one who is not imprisoned, "Why am I here?" His appeal is audible in Heaven; and will become audible enough on Earth too, if it remain unheeded here. His appeal is against you, foremost of all; you stand in the front rank of the accused; you, by the very place you hold, have first of all to answer him and Heaven!

What looks maddest, miserablest in these mad and miserable Corn-Laws is independent altogether of their 'effect on wages,' their effect on 'increase of trade,' or any other such effect: it is the continual maddening proof they protrude into the faces of all men, that our Governing Class, called by God and Nature and the inflexible law of Fact, either to do something towards governing, or to die and be abolished,—have not yet learned even to sit still, and do no mischief! For no Anti-Corn-Law League yet asks more of them than this;—Nature and Fact, very imperatively, asking so much more of them. Anti-Corn-Law League asks not, Do something; but, Cease your destructive misdoing, Do ye nothing!

Nature's message will have itself obeyed: messages of mere Free-Trade, Anti-Corn-Law League and Laissez-faire, will then need small obeying!—Ye fools, in the name of Heaven, work, work, at the Ark of Deliverance for yourselves and us, while hours are still granted you! No: instead of working at the Ark, they say, "We cannot get our hands kept rightly warm;" and *sit obstinately burning the planks.* No madder spectacle at present exhibits itself under this Sun.

The Working Aristocracy; Mill-owners, Manufacturers, Commanders of Working Men: alas, against them also much shall be brought in accusation; much,—and the freest Trade in Corn, total abolition of Tariffs, and uttermost 'Increase of Manufactures' and 'Prosperity of Commerce,' will permanently mend no jot of it. The Working Aristocracy must strike into a new path; must understand that money alone is *not* the representative either of man's success in the world, or of man's duties to man; and reform their own selves from top to bottom, if they wish England reformed. England will not be habitable long unreformed.

The Working Aristocracy—Yes, but on the threshold of all this, it is again and again to be asked, What of the Idle Aristocracy? Again and again, What shall we say of the Idle Aristocracy, the Owners of the Soil of England; whose recognised function is that of handsomely consuming the rents of England, shooting the partridges of England, and as an agreeable amusement (if the purchase-money and other conveniences serve), dilettante-ing in Parliament and Quarter-Sessions for England? We will say mournfully, in the presence of Heaven and Earth,—that we stand speechless, stupent, and know not what to say! That a class of men entitled to live sumptuously on the marrow of the earth; permitted simply, nay entreated, and as yet entreated in vain, to do nothing at all in return, was never heretofore seen on the face of this Planet. That such a class is transitory, exceptional, and, unless Nature's Laws fall dead, cannot continue. That it has continued now a moderate while; has, for the last fifty years, been rapidly attaining its state of perfection. That it will have to find its duties and do them; or else that it must and will cease to be seen on the face of this Planet, which is a Working one, not an Idle one.

Alas, alas, the Working Aristocracy, admonished by Trades-unions, Chartist conflagrations, above all by their own shrewd sense kept in perpetual communion with the fact of things, will assuredly reform themselves, and a working world will still be possible:—but the fate of the Idle Aristocracy, as one reads its horoscope hitherto in Corn-Laws and such like, is an abyss that fills one with despair. Yes, my rosy fox-hunting brothers, a terrible *Hippocratic look* reveals itself (God knows, not to my joy) through those fresh buxom countenances of yours. Through your Corn-Law Majorities, Sliding-Scales, Protecting-Duties, Bribery-Elections and triumphant Kentish-fire, a thinking eye discerns ghastly, images of ruin, too ghastly for words; a handwriting as of MENE, MENE. Men and brothers, on your Sliding-scale you seem sliding, and to have slid,—you little know whither! Good God! did not a French Donothing Aristocracy, hardly above half a century ago, declare in like manner, and in its featherhead believe in like manner, "We cannot exist, and continue to dress and parade ourselves, on the just rent of the soil of France; but we must have farther payment than rent of the soil, we must be exempted from taxes too,"—we must have a Corn-Law to extend our rent? This was in 1789: in four years more—Did you look into the Tanneries of Meudon, and the long-naked making for themselves breeches of human skins! May the merciful Heavens avert the omen; may we be wiser, that so we be less wretched.

A High Class without duties to do is like a tree planted on precipices; from the roots of which all the earth has been crumbling. Nature owns no man who is not a Martyr withal. Is there a man who pretends to live luxuriously housed up; screened from all work, from want, danger, hardships, the victory over which is what we name work;—he himself to sit serene, amid down-bolsters and appliances, and have all his work and battling done by other men? And such man calls himself a *noble*-man? His fathers worked for him, he says; or successfully gambled for him: here *he* sits; professes, not in sorrow but in pride, that he and his have done no work, time out of mind. It is the law of the land, and is thought to be the law of the Universe, that he, alone of recorded men, shall have no task laid on him, except that of eating his cooked victuals, and not flinging himself out of window. Once more I will say, there was no stranger spectacle ever shewn under this Sun. A veritable fact in our England of the Nineteenth Century. His victuals he does eat: but as for keeping in the inside of the window,—have not his friends, like me, enough to do? Truly, looking at his Corn-Laws, Game-Laws, Chandos-Clauses, Bribery-Elections and much else, you do shudder over the tumbling and plunging he makes, held back by the lappelles and coatskirts; only a thin fence of window-glass before him,—and in the street mere horrid iron spikes! My sick brother, as in hospital-maladies men do, thou dreamest of Paradises and Eldorados, which are far from thee. 'Cannot I do what I like with my own?' Gracious Heaven, my brother, this that thou seest with those sick eyes is no firm Eldorado, and Corn-Law Paradise of Donothings, but a dream of thy own fevered brain. It is a glass-window, I tell thee, so many stories from the street; where are iron spikes and the law of gravitation!

What is the meaning of nobleness, if this be 'noble?' In a valiant suffering for others, not in a slothful making others suffer for us, did nobleness ever lie. The chief of men is he who stands in the van of men; fronting the peril which frightens back all others; which, if it be not vanquished, will devour the others. Every noble crown is, and on Earth will forever be, a crown of thorns. The Pagan Hercules, why was he accounted a hero? Because he had slain Nemean Lions, cleansed Augean Stables, undergone Twelve Labours only not too heavy for a god. In modern, as in ancient and all societies, the Aristocracy, they that assume the functions of an Aristocracy, doing them or not, have taken the post of honour; which is the post of difficulty, the post of danger,—of death, if the difficulty be not overcome. *Il faut payer de sa vie* ["you must pay with your life"]. Why was our life given us, if not that we should manfully give it? Descend, O Donothing Pomp: quit thy down-cushions; expose thyself to learn what wretches feel, and how to cure it! The Czar of Russia became a dusty toiling shipwright; worked with his axe in the Docks of Saardam; and his aim was small to thine. Descend thou: undertake this horrid 'living chaos of Ignorance and Hunger' weltering round thy feet; say, "I will heal it, or behold I will die foremost in it." Such is verily the law. Everywhere and everywhen a man has to '*pay* with his life;' to do his work, as a soldier does, at the expense of life. In no Piepowder earthly Court can you sue an Aristocracy to do its work, at this moment: but in the Higher Court, which even *it* calls 'Court of Honour,' and which is the Court of Necessity withal, and the eternal Court of the Universe, in which all Facts comes to plead, and every Human Soul is an apparitor,—the Aristocracy is answerable, and even now answering, *there*.

Parchments? Parchments are venerable: but they ought at all

The Modern Worker

times to represent, as near as they by possibility can, the writing of the Adamant Tablets; otherwise they are not so venerable! Benedict the Jew in vain pleaded parchments; his usuries were too many. The King said, "Go to, for all thy parchments, thou shalt pay just debt; down with thy dust, or observe this tooth-forceps!" Nature, a far juster Sovereign, has far terribler forceps!" Aristocracies, actual and imaginary, reach a time when parchment pleading does not avail them. "Go to, for all thy parchments, thou shalt pay due debt!" shouts the Universe to them, in an emphatic manner. They refuse to pay, confidently pleading parchment: their best grinder-tooth, with horrible agony, goes out of their jaw. Wilt thou pay now? A second grinder, again in horrible agony, goes: a second, and a third, and if need be, all the teeth and grinders, and the life itself with them;—and *then* there is free payment, and an anatomist subject into the bargain!

Reform Bills, Corn-Law Abrogation Bills, and then Land-Tax Bill, Property-Tax Bill, and still dimmer list of *etceteras*; grinder after grinder:—my lords and gentlemen, it were better for you to arise, and begin doing your work, than sit there and plead parchments!

We write no chapter on the Corn-Laws, in this place; the Corn-Laws are too mad to have a Chapter. There is a certain immorality, when there is not a necessity, in speaking about things finished; in chopping into small pieces the already slashed and slain. When the brains are out, why does not a Solecism die! It is at its own peril if it refuse to die; it ought to make all conceivable haste to die, and get itself buried! The trade of Anti-Corn-Law Lecturer in these days, still an indispensable, is a highly tragic one.

The Corn-Laws will go, and even soon go: would we were all as sure of the Millennium as they are of going! They go swiftly in these present months; with an increase of velocity, an ever-deepening, ever-widening sweep of momentum, truly notable. It is at the Aristocracy's own damage and peril, still more than at any other's whatsoever, that the Aristocracy maintains them;—at a damage, say only, as above computed, of a 'hundred thousand pounds an hour!' The Corn-Laws keep all the air hot-fostered by their fever-warmth, much that is evil, but much also, how much that is good and indispensable, is rapidly coming to life among us!

IX: Working Aristocracy

A POOR Working Mammonism getting itself 'strangled in the partridge-nets of an Unworking Dilettantism,' and bellowing dreadfully, and already black in the face, is surely a disastrous spectacle! But of a Midas-eared Mammonism, which indeed at bottom all pure Mammonisms are, what better can you expect? No better;—if not this, then something other equally disastrous, if not still more disastrous. Mammonisms, grown asinine, have to become human again, and rational; they have, on the whole, to cease to be Mammonisms, were it even on compulsion, and pressure of the hemp round their neck!— My friends of the Working Aristocracy, there are now a great many things which you also, in your extreme need, will have to consider.

The Continental people, it would seem, are 'exporting our machinery, beginning to spin cotton and manufacture for themselves, to cut us out of this market and then out of that!' Sad news indeed; but irremediable;—by no means the saddest news. The saddest news is, that we should find our National Existence, as I sometimes hear it said, depend on selling manufactured cotton at a farthing an ell cheaper than any other People. A most narrow stand for a great Nation to base itself on! A stand which, with all the Corn-Law Abrogations conceivable, I do not think will be capable of enduring. My friends, suppose we quitted that stand; suppose we came honestly down from it, and said: "This is our minimum of cotton-prices. We care not, for the present, to make cotton any cheaper. Do you, if it seem so blessed to you, make cotton cheaper. Fill your lungs with cotton-fuz, your hearts with copperas-fumes, with rage and mutiny; become ye the general gnomes of Europe, slaves of the lamp!"—I admire a Nation which fancies it will die if it do not undersell all other Nations, to the end of the world. Brothers, we will cease to *under*sell them; we will be content to *equal*-sell them; to be happy selling equally with them! I do not see the use of underselling them. Cotton-cloth is already two-pence a yard or lower; and yet bare backs were never more numerous among us. Let inventive men cease to spend their existence incessantly contriving how cotton can be made cheaper; and try to invent, a little, how cotton at its present cheapness could be somewhat justlier divided among us. Let inventive men consider, Whether the Secret of this Universe, and of Man's Life there, does, after all, as we rashly fancy it, consist in making money? There is One God, just, supreme, almighty: but is Mammon the name of him?—With a Hell which means 'Failing to make money,' I do not think there is any Heaven possible that would suit one well; nor so much as an Earth that can be habitable long! In brief, all this Mammon-Gospel, of Supply-and-demand, Competition, Laissez-faire, and Devil take the hindmost, begins to be one of the shabbiest Gospels ever preached; or altogether the shabbiest. Even with Dilettante partridge-nets, and at a horrible expenditure of pain, who shall regret to see the entirely transient, and at best somewhat despicable life strangled out of it? At the best, as we say, a somewhat despicable, unvenerable thing, this same 'Laissez-faire;' and now, at the *worst*, fast growing an altogether detestable one!

"But what is to be done with our manufacturing population, with our agricultural, with our ever-increasing population?" cry many.—Aye, what? Many things can be done with them, a hundred things, and a thousand things,—had we once got a soul and begun to try. This one thing, of doing for them by 'underselling all people' and filling our own bursten pockets and appetites by the road; and turning over all care for any 'population,' or human or divine consideration except cash only, to the winds, with a "Laissez-faire" and the rest of it: this is evidently not the thing. Farthing cheaper per yard? No great Nation can stand on the apex of such a pyramid; screwing itself higher and higher; balancing itself on its great-toe! Can England not subsist without being *above* all people in working? England never deliberately purposed such a thing. If England work better than all people, it shall be well. England, like an honest worker, will work as well as she can; and hope the gods may allow her to live on that basis. Laissez-faire and much else being once well dead, how many 'impossibles' will become possible! They are impossible, as cotton-cloth at two-pence an ell was—till men set about making it. The inventive genius of great England will not forever sit patient with mere wheels and pinions, bobbins, straps and billy-rollers whirring in the head of it. The inventive genius of England is not a Beaver's, or a Spinner's or Spider's genius: it is a *Man's* genius, I hope, with a God over him!

Laissez-faire, Supply-and-demand,—one begins to be weary of all that. Leave all to egoism, to ravenous greed of money, of pleasure, of applause;—it is the Gospel of Despair! Man is a Patent-Digester, then: only give him Free Trade, Free digesting room; and each of us digest what he can come at, leaving the rest to Fate! My unhappy brethren of the Working Mammonism, my unhappy brethren of the Idle Dilettantism, no world was ever held together in that way for long. A world of mere Patent-Digesters will soon have nothing to digest; such world ends, and by Law of Nature must end, in 'over-population;' in howling universal famine, 'impossibility,' and suicidal madness, as of endless dog-kennels run rabid. Supply-and-demand shall do its full part, and Free Trade shall be free as air; thou of the shotbelts, see thou forbid it not, with those paltry, *worse* than Mammonish swindleries and Sliding-scales of thine, which are seen to be swindleries for all thy canting, which in times like ours are very scandalous to see! And trade never so well freed, and all Tariffs settled or abolished, and Supply-and-demand in full operation,—let us all know that we have yet done nothing; that we have merely cleared the ground for doing.

Yes, were the Corn-Laws ended tomorrow, there is nothing yet ended; there is only room made for all manner of things beginning. The Corn-Laws gone, and Trade made free, it is as good as certain this paralysis of industry will pass away. We shall have another period of commercial enterprise, of victory and prosperity; during which, it is likely, much money will again be made, and all the people may, by the extant methods, still for a space of years, be kept alive and physically fed. The strangling band of Famine will be loosened from our necks; we shall have room again to breathe; time to bethink ourselves, to repeat and consider! A precious and thrice-precious space of years; wherein to struggle as for life in reforming our foul ways; in alleviating, instructing, regulating our people; seeking as for life, that something like spiritual food be imparted them, some real governance and guidance be provided them! It will be a priceless time. For our new period or paroxysm of commercial prosperity will and can, on the old methods of 'Competition and Devil take the hindmost,' prove but a paroxysm: a new paroxysm,—likely enough, if we do not use it better, to be our *last*. In tins, of itself, is no salvation. If our Trade in twenty years' 'flourishing' as never Trade flourished, could double itself; yet then also, by the old Laissez-faire method, our Population is doubled: we shall then be as we are, only twice as many of us, twice and ten times as unmanageable!

All this dire misery, therefore; all this of our poor Workhouse Workmen, of our Chartisms, Trades-strikes, Corn-Laws, Toryisms, and the general downbreak of Laissez-faire in these days,—may we not regard it as a voice from the dumb bosom of Nature, saying to us: "Behold! Supply-and-demand is not the one Law of Nature; Cash-payment is not the sole nexus of man with man,—how far from it! Deep, far deeper than Supply-and-demand, are Laws, Obligations sacred as Man's Life itself: these also, if you will continue to do work, you shall now learn and obey. He that will learn them, behold Nature is on his side, he shall yet work and prosper with noble rewards. He that will not learn them, Nature is against him, he shall not be able to do work in Nature's empire,—not in hers. Perpetual mutiny, contention, hatred, isolation, execration shall wait on his footsteps, till all men discern that the thing which he attains; however golden it look or be, is not success, but the want of success."

Supply-and-demand,—alas! For what noble work was there ever yet any audible 'demand' in that poor sense? The man of Macedonia, speaking in vision to an Apostle Paul, "Come over and help us," did not specify what rate of wages he would give! Or was the Christian Religion itself accomplished by Prize-Essays, Bridgewater Bequests, and a 'minimum of Four thousand five hundred a year'? No demand that I heard of was made then, audible in any Labour-market, Manchester Chamber of Commerce, or other the like emporium and hiring establishment; silent were all these from any whisper of such demand;—powerless were all these to 'supply' it, had the demand been in thunder and earthquake, with gold Eldorados and Mahometan Paradises for the reward.

Ah me, into what waste latitudes, in this Time-Voyage, have we wandered; like adventurous Sindbads;—where the men go about as if by galvanism, with meaningless glaring eyes, and have no soul, but only a beaver-faculty and stomach! The haggard despair of Cotton-factory, Coal-mine operatives, Chandos Farm-labourers, in these days, is painful to behold; but not so painful, hideous to the inner sense, as that brutish godforgetting Profit-and-Loss Philosophy, and Life-theory, which we hear jangled on all hands of us, in senate-houses, spouting-clubs, leading-articles, pulpits and platforms, everywhere, as the Ultimate Gospel and candid Plain-English of Man's Life, from the throats and pens and thoughts of all but all men!—

Enlightened Philosophies, like Molière Doctors, will tell you: "Enthusiasms, Self-sacrifice, Heaven, Hell and such like: yes, all that was true enough for old stupid times; all that used to be true: but we have changed all that, *nous avons changé tout cela!*" Well; if the heart be got round now into the right side, and the liver to the left; if man have no heroism in him deeper than a wish to eat, and in his soul there dwell now no Infinite of Hope and Awe, and no divine Silence can become imperative because it is not Sinai Thunder, and no tie will bind if it be not that of Tyburn gallows-ropes,—then verily you have changed all that; and for it, and for you, and for me, behold the Abyss and nameless Annihilation is ready. So scandalous a beggarly Universe deserves indeed nothing else; I cannot say I would save it from annihilation. Vacuum, and the serene Blue, will be much handsomer; easier too for all of us. I, for one, decline living as a Patent-Digester. Patent-Digester, Spinning-Mule, Mayfair Clothes-Horse: many thanks, but your Chaosships will have the goodness to excuse me!

X: Plugson of Undershot

One thing I do know: Never, on this Earth was the relation of man to man long carried on by Cash-payment alone. If, at any time, a philosophy of Laissez-faire, Competition and Supply-and-demand, start up as the exponent of human relations, expect that it will soon end.

Such philosophies will arise: for man's philosophies are usually the 'supplement of his practice;' some ornamental Logic-varnish, some outer skin of Articulate Intelligence, with which he strives to render his dumb Instinctive doings presentable when they are done. Such philosophies will arise; be preached as Mammon-Gospels, the ultimate Evangel of the World; be believed, with what is called belief, with much superficial bluster, and a kind of shallow satisfaction real in its way:—but they are ominous gospels! They are the sure, and even swift forerunner of great changes. Expect that the old System of Society is done, is dying and falling into dotage, when it begins to rave in that fashion. Most Systems that I have watched the death of, for the last three thousand years, have gone just so. The Ideal, the True and Noble that was in them having faded out, and nothing now remaining but naked Egoism, vulturous Greediness, they cannot live; they are bound and inexorably ordained by the oldest Destinies, Mothers of the Universe, to die. Curious enough; they thereupon, as I have pretty generally noticed, devise some light comfortable kind of 'wine-and-walnuts philosophy' for themselves, this of Supply-and-demand or another; and keep saying, during hours of mastication and rumination, which they call hours of meditation: "Soul, take thy ease, it is all *well* that thou art a vulture-soul;"—and pangs of dissolution come upon them, oftenest before they are aware!

Cash-payment never was, or could except for a few years be, the union-bond of man to man. Cash never yet paid one man fully his deserts to another; nor could it, nor can it, now or henceforth to the end of the world. I invite his Grace of Castle Rack-rent to reflect on this,—does he think that a Land Aristocracy when it becomes a Land Auctioneership can have long to live? Or that Sliding-scales will increase the vital stamina of it?—The indomitable Plugson too, of the respected Firm of Plugson, Hunks and Company, in St. Dolly Undershot, is invited to reflect on this; for to him also it will be new, perhaps even newer. Bookkeeping by double entry is admirable, and records several things in an exact manner. But the Mother-Destinies also keep their Tablets; in Heaven's Chancery also there goes on a recording; and things, as my Moslem friends say, are 'written on the iron-leaf.'

Your Grace and Plugson, it is like, go to Church occasionally: did you never in vacant moments, with perhaps a dull parson droning to you, glance into your New Testament, and the cash-account stated four times over, by a kind of quadruple entry,—in the Four Gospels there? I consider that a cash account, and balance-statement of work done and wages paid, worth attending to. Precisely *such*, though on a smaller scale, go on at all moments under this Sun; and the statement and balance of them in the Plugson Ledgers and on the Tablets of Heaven's Chancery are discrepant exceedingly;—which ought really to teach, and to have long since taught, an indomitable common-sense Plugson of Undershot, much more an unattackable *un*common-sense Grace of Rack-rent, a thing or two!—In brief, we shall have to dismiss the Cash-Gospel rigorously into its own place: we shall have to know, on the threshold, that either there is some infinitely deeper Gospel, subsidiary, explanatory and daily and hourly corrective, to the Cash one; or else that the Cash one itself and all others are fast travelling!

For all human things do require to have an Ideal in them; to have some Soul in them, as we said, were it only to keep the Body unputrefied. And wonderful it is to see how the Ideal or Soul, place it in what ugliest Body you may, will irradiate said Body with its own nobleness; will gradually, incessantly, mould, modify new-form or reform said ugliest Body, and make it at last beautiful, and to a certain degree divine! O, if you could dethrone that Brute-god Mammon, and put a Spirit-god in his place! One way or other, he must and will have to be dethroned.

Fighting, for example, as I often say to myself, Fighting with steel murder-tools is surely a much uglier operation than Working, take it how you will. Yet even of Fighting, in religious Abbot Samson's days, see what a Feudalism there had grown,—a 'glorious Chivalry,' much besung down to the present day. Was not that one of the 'impossiblest' things? Under the sky is no uglier spectacle than two men with clenched teeth, and hellfire eyes, hacking one another's flesh; converting precious living bodies, and priceless living souls, into nameless masses of putrescence, useful only for turnip-manure. How did a Chivalry ever come out of that; how anything that was not hideous, scandalous, infernal? It will be a question worth considering by and by.

I remark, for the present, only two things: first, that the Fighting itself was not, as we rashly suppose it, a Fighting without cause, but more or less with cause. Man is created to fight; he is perhaps best of all definable as a born-soldier; his life 'a battle and a march,' under the right General. It is forever indispensable for a man to fight: now with Necessity, with Barrenness, Scarcity, with Puddles, Bogs, tangled Forests, unkempt Cotton;—now also with the hallucinations of his poor fellow Men. Hallucinatory visions rise in the head of my poor fellow man; make him claim over me rights which are not his. All Fighting, as we noticed long ago, is the dusty conflict of strengths, each thinking itself the strongest, or, in other words, the justest;—of Mights which do in the long-run, and forever will in this just Universe in the long-run, mean Rights. In conflict the perishable part of them, beaten sufficiently, flies off into dust: this process ended, appears the imperishable, the true and exact.

And now let us remark a second thing: how, in these baleful operations, a noble devout-hearted Chevalier will comfort himself, and an ignoble godless Bucanier and Chactaw Indian. Victory is the aim of each. But deep in the heart of the noble man it lies forever legible, that, as an Invisible Just God made him, so will and must God's Justice and this only, were it never so invisible, ultimately prosper in all controversies and enterprises and battles whatsoever. What an Influence; ever-present,—like a Soul in the rudest Caliban of a body; like a ray of Heaven, and illuminative creative *Fiat-Lux* ["let there be light"], in the wastest terrestrial Chaos! Blessed divine Influence, traceable even in the horror of Battlefields and garments rolled in blood: how it ennobles even the Battlefield; and, in place of a Chactaw Massacre, makes it a Field of Honour! A Battlefield too is great. Considered well, it is a kind of Quintessence of Labour; Labour distilled into its utmost concentration; the significance of years of it compressed into an hour. Here too thou shalt be strong, and not in muscle only, if thou wouldst prevail. Here too thou shalt be strong of heart, noble of soul; thou shalt dread no pain or death, thou shalt not love ease or life; in rage, thou shalt remember mercy, justice;—thou shalt be a Knight and not a Chactaw, if thou wouldst prevail! It is the rule of all battles, against hallucinating fellow Men, against unkempt Cotton, or whatsoever battles they may be, which a man in this world has to fight.

Howel Davies dyes the West Indian Seas with blood, piles his decks with plunder; approves himself the expertest Seaman, the daringest Seafighter: but he gains no lasting victory, lasting victory is not possible for him. Not, had he fleets larger than the combined British Navy all united with him in bucaniering. He, once for all, cannot prosper in his duel. He strikes down his man: yes; but his man, or his man's representative, has no notion to lie struck down: neither, though slain ten times, will he keep so lying;—nor has the Universe any notion to keep him so lying! On the contrary, the Universe and he have, at all moments, all manner of motives to start up again, and desperately fight again. Your Napoleon is flung out, at last to St. Helena; the latter end of him sternly compensating the beginning. The Bucanier strikes down a man, a hundred or a million men: but what profits it? He has one enemy never to be struck down; nay two enemies: Mankind and the Maker of Men. On the great scale or on the small, in fighting of men or fighting of difficulties, I will not embark my venture with Howel Davies: it is not the Bucanier, it is the Hero only that can gain victory, that can do more than *seem* to succeed. These things will deserve meditating; for they apply to all battle and soldiership, all struggle and effort whatsoever in this Fight of Life. It is a poor Gospel, Cash-Gospel or whatever name it have, that does not, with clear tone, uncontradictable, carrying conviction to all hearts, forever keep men in mind of these things.

Unhappily, my indomitable friend Plugson of Undershot has, in a great degree, forgotten them;—as, alas, all the world has; as, alas, our very Dukes and Soul-Overseers have, whose special trade it was to remember them! Hence these tears.— Plugson, who has indomitably spun Cotton merely to gain thousands of pounds, I have to call as yet a Bucanier and Chactaw; till there come something better, still more indomitable from him. His hundred Thousand-pound Notes, if there be nothing other, are to me but as the hundred Scalps in a Chactaw wigwam. The blind Plugson; he was a Captain of Industry, born member of the Ultimate genuine Aristocracy of this Universe, could he have known it! These thousand men that span and toiled round him, they were a regiment whom he had enlisted, man by man; to make war on a very genuine enemy: Bareness of back, and disobedient Cotton-fibre, which will not, unless forced to it, consent to cover bare backs. Here is a most genuine enemy; over whom all creatures will wish him victory. He enlisted his thousand men; said to them, "Come, brothers, let us have a dash at Cotton!" They follow with cheerful shout; they gain such a victory over Cotton as the Earth has to admire and clap hands at: but, alas, it is yet only of the Bucanier or Chactaw sort,—as good as no victory! Foolish Plugson of St. Dolly Undershot: does he hope to become illustrious by hanging up the scalps in his wigwam, the hundred thousands at his banker's, and saying, Behold my scalps? Why Plugson, even thy own host is all in mutiny: Cotton is conquered; but the 'bare backs'—are worse covered than ever! Indomitable Plugson, thou must cease to be a Chactaw; thou and others; thou thyself, if no other!

Did William the Norman Bastard, or any of his Taillefers, *Ironcutters*, manage so? Ironcutter, at the end of the campaign, did not turn off his thousand fighters, but said to them: "Noble fighters, this is the land we have gained; be I Lord in it,—what we will call *Law-ward*, maintainer and *keeper* of Heaven's *Laws*: be I *Law-ward*, or in brief orthoepy *Lord* in it, and be ye Loyal Men around me in it; and we will stand by one another, as soldiers round a captain, for again we shall have need of one another!" Plugson, bucanier-like, says to them: "Noble spinners, this is the Hundred Thousand we have gained, wherein I mean to dwell and plant vineyards; the hundred thousand is mine, the three and sixpence daily was yours: adieu, noble spinners; drink my health with this groat each, which I give you over and above!" The entirely unjust Captain of Industry, say I; not Chevalier, but Bucanier!

'Commercial Law' does indeed acquit him; asks, with wide eyes, What else? So too Howel Davies asks, Was it not according to the strictest Bucanier Custom? Did I depart in any jot or tittle from the Laws of the Bucaniers?

After all, money, as they say, is miraculous. Plugson wanted victory; as Chevaliers and Bucaniers, and all men alike do. He found money recognised by the whole world with one assent, as the true symbol, exact equivalent and synonym of victory;—and here we have him, a grimbrowed indomitable Bucanier, coming home to us with a 'victory' which the whole world is *ceasing* to clap hands at! The whole world, taught somewhat impressively, is beginning to recognise that such victory is but half a victory; and that now, if it please the Powers, we must—have the other half!

Money is miraculous. What miraculous facilities has it yielded, will it yield us; but also what never-imagined confusions, obscurations has it brought in; down almost to total extinction of the moral-sense in large masses of mankind! 'Protection of property,' of what is '*mine*,' means with most men protection of money,—the thing which, had I a thousand padlocks over it, is least of all *mine*; is, in a manner, scarcely worth calling mine! The symbol shall be held sacred, defended everywhere with tipstaves, ropes and gibbets; the thing signified shall be composedly cast to the dogs. A human being who has worked with human beings clears all scores with them, cuts himself with triumphant completeness forever loose from them, by paying down certain shillings and pounds. Was it not the wages I promised you? There they are, to the last sixpence,—according to the Laws of the Bucaniers!—Yes, indeed;—and, at such times, it becomes imperatively necessary to ask all persons, bucaniers and others, Whether these same respectable Laws of the Bucaniers are written on God's eternal Heavens at all, on the inner Heart of Man at all; or on the respectable Bucaniers Logbook merely, for the convenience of bucaniering merely? What a question;—whereat Westminster Hall shudders to its driest parchment; and on the dead wigs each particular horse-hair stands on end!

The Laws of Laissez-faire, O Westminster, the laws of industrial Captain and industrial Soldier, how much more of idle Captain and industrial Soldier, will need to be remodelled, and modified, and rectified in a hundred and a hundred ways,—and *not* in the Sliding scale direction, but in the totally opposite one! With two million industrial Soldiers already sitting in Bastilles, and five millions pining on potatoes, methinks Westminster cannot begin too soon!—A man has other obligations laid on him in God's Universe, than the payment of cash: these also Westminster, if it will continue to exist and have board-wages, must contrive to take some charge of:—by Westminster or by another, they must and will be taken charge of; be, with whatever difficulty, got articulated, got enforced, and to a certain approximate extent, put in practice. And, as I say, it cannot be too soon! For Mammonism, left to itself, has become Midas-eared; and with all its gold mountains, sits starving for want of bread: and Dilettantism with its partridge-nets, in this extremely earnest Universe of ours, is playing somewhat too high a game. 'A man by the very look of him promises so much:' yes; and by the rent-roll of him does he promise nothing?—

Alas, what a business will this be, which our Continental friends, groping this long while somewhat absurdly about it and about it, call 'Organisation of Labour—which must be taken out of the hands of absurd windy persons, and put into the hands of wise, laborious, modest and valiant men, to begin with it straightway: to proceed with it, and succeed in it more and more, if Europe, at any rate if England, is to continue habitable much longer. Looking at the kind of most noble Corn-Law Dukes or Practical *Duces* we have, and also of right reverend Soul-Overseers, Christian Spiritual *Duces* 'on a minimum of four thousand five hundred,' one's hopes are a little chilled. Courage, nevertheless; there are many brave men in England! My indomitable Plugson,—nay is there not even in thee some hope? Thou art hitherto a Bucanier, as it was written and prescribed for thee by an evil world: but in that grim brow, in that indomitable heart which *can* conquer Cotton, do there not perhaps lie other ten-times nobler conquests?

XI: Labour

For there is a perennial nobleness, and even sacredness, in Work. Were he never so benighted, forgetful of his high calling, there is always hope in a man that actually and earnestly works: in Idleness alone is there perpetual despair. Work, never so Mammonish, mean, *is* in communication with Nature; the real desire to get Work done will itself lead one more and more to truth, to Nature's appointments and regulations, which are truth.

The latest Gospel in this world is, Know thy work and do it. 'Know thyself:' long enough has that poor 'self' of thine tormented thee; thou wilt never get to 'know' it, I believe! Think it not thy business, this of knowing thyself; thou art an unknowable individual: know what thou canst work at; and work at it, like a Hercules! That will be thy better plan.

It has been written, 'an endless significance lies in Work;' a man perfects himself by working. Foul jungles are cleared away, fair seedfields rise instead, and stately cities; and withal the man himself first ceases to be jungle and foul unwholesome desert thereby. Consider how, even in the meanest sorts of Labour, the whole soul of a man is composed into a kind of real harmony, the instant he sets himself to work! Doubt, Desire, Sorrow, Remorse, Indignation, Despair itself, all these like hell-dogs lie beleaguering the soul of the poor dayworker, as of every man: but he bends himself with free valour against his task, and all these are stilled, all these shrink murmuring far off into their caves. The man is now a man. The blessed glow of Labour in him, is it not as purifying fire, wherein all poison is burnt up, and of sour smoke itself there is made bright blessed flame!

Destiny, on the whole, has no other way of cultivating us. A formless Chaos once set it *revolving*, grows round and even rounder; ranges itself, by mere force of gravity, into strata, spherical courses; is no longer a Chaos, but a round compacted World. What would become of the Earth, did she cease to revolve? In the poor old Earth, so long as she revolves, all inequalities, irregularities disperse themselves; all irregularities are incessantly becoming regular. Hast thou looked on the Potter's wheel,—one of the venerablest objects; old as the Prophet Ezechiel and far older? Rude lumps of clay, how they spin themselves up, by mere quick whirling, into beautiful circular dishes. And fancy the most assiduous Potter, but without his wheel; reduced to make dishes, or rather amorphous botches, by mere kneading and baking! Even such a Potter were Destiny, with a human soul that would rest and lie at ease, that would not work and spin! Of an idle unrevolving man the kindest Destiny, like the most assiduous Potter without wheel, can bake and knead nothing other than a botch; let her spend on him what expensive colouring, what gilding and enamelling she will, he is but a botch. Not a dish; no, a bulging, kneaded, crooked, shambling, squint-cornered, amorphous botch,—a mere enamelled vessel of dishonour! Let the idle think of this.

Blessed is he who has found his work; let him ask no other blessedness. He has a work, a life-purpose; he has found it, and will follow it! How, as a free-flowing channel, dug and torn by noble force through the sour mud-swamp of one's existence, like an ever-deepening river there, it runs and flows;—draining off the sour festering water, gradually from the root of the remotest grass-blade; making, instead of pestilential swamp, a green fruitful meadow with its clear-flowing stream. How blessed for the meadow itself, let the stream and *its* value be great or small! Labour is Life: from the inmost heart of the Worker rises his god-given Force, the sacred celestial Life-essence breathed into him by Almighty God; from his inmost heart awakens him to all nobleness,—to all knowledge, 'self-knowledge' and much else, so soon as Work fitly begins. Knowledge? The knowledge that will hold good in working, cleave thou to that; for Nature herself accredits that, says Yea to that. Properly thou hast no other knowledge but what thou hast got by working: the rest is yet all a hypothesis of knowledge; a thing to be argued of in schools, a thing floating in the clouds, in endless logic-vortices, till we try it and fix it. 'Doubt, of whatever kind, can be ended by Action alone.'

And again, hast thou valued Patience, Courage, Perseverance, Openness to light; readiness to own thyself mistaken, to do better next time? All these, all virtues, in wrestling with the dim brute Powers of Fact, in ordering of thy fellows in such wrestle, there and elsewhere not at all, thou wilt continually learn. Set down a brave Sir Christopher in the middle of black ruined Stoneheaps, of foolish unarchitectural Bishops, redtape Officials, idle Nell-Gwyn Defenders of the Faith; and see whether he will ever raise a Paul's Cathedral out of all that, yea or no! Rough, rude, contradictory are all things and persons, from the mutinous masons and Irish hodmen, up to the idle Nell-Gwyn Defenders, to blustering redtape Officials, foolish unarchitectural Bishops. All these things and persons are there not for Christopher's sake and his Cathedral's; they are there for their own sake mainly! Christopher will have to conquer and constrain all these,—if he be able. All these are against him. Equitable Nature herself, who carries her mathematics and architectonics not on the face of her, but deep in the hidden heart of her,—Nature herself is but partially for him; will be wholly against him, if he constrain her not! His very money, where is it to come from? The pious munificence of England lies far-scattered, distant, unable to speak, and say, "I am here;"—must be spoken to before it can speak. Pious munificence, and all help, is so silent, invisible like the gods; impediment, contradictions manifold are so loud and near! O brave Sir Christopher, trust thou in those, notwithstanding, and front all these; understand all these; by valiant patience, noble effort, insight, by man's-strength, vanquish and compel all these,—and, on the whole, strike down victoriously the last topstone of that Paul's Edifice; thy monument for certain centuries, the stamp 'Great Man' impressed very legibly on Portland-stone there!—

Yes, all manner of help, and pious response from Men of Nature, is always what we call silent; cannot speak or come to light, till it be seen, till it be spoken to. Every noble work is at first 'impossible.' In very truth, for every noble work the possibilities will lie diffused through Immensity; inarticulate, undiscoverable except to faith. Like Gideon thou shalt spread out thy fleece at the door of thy tent; see whether under the wide arch of Heaven there be any bounteous moisture, or none. Thy heart and life-purpose shall be as a miraculous

Gideon's fleece, spread out in silent appeal to Heaven; and from the kind Immensities, what from the poor unkind Localities and town and country Parishes there never could, blessed dew-moisture to suffice thee shall have fallen!

Work is of a religious nature:—work is of a *brave* nature; which it is the aim of all religion to be. All work of man is as the swimmer's; a waste ocean threatens to devour him; if he front it not bravely, it will keep its word. By incessant wise defiance of it, lusty rebuke and buffet of it, behold how it loyally supports him, bears him as its conqueror along. 'It is so,' says Goethe, 'with all things that man undertakes in this world.'

Brave Sea-captain, Norse Sea-king,—Columbus, my hero, royalest Sea-king of all! it is no friendly environment this of thine, in the waste deep waters; around thee mutinous discouraged souls, behind thee disgrace and ruin, before thee the unpenetrated veil of Night. Brother, these wild water-mountains, bounding from their deep basin (ten miles deep, I am told), are not entirely there on thy behalf! Meseems *they* have other work than floating thee forward:—and the huge Winds, that sweep from Ursa Major to the Tropics and Equators, dancing their giant-waltz through the kingdoms of Chaos and Immensity, they care little about filling rightly or filling wrongly the small shoulder-of-mutton sails in this cockle-skiff of thine! Thou are not among articulate-speaking friends, my brother; thou art among immeasurable dumb monsters, tumbling, howling wide as the world here. Secret, far off, invisible to all hearts but thine, there lies a help in them: see how thou wilt get at that. Patiently thou wilt wait till the mad South-wester spend itself, saving thyself by dexterous science of defence, the while: valiantly, with swift decision, wilt thou strike in, when the favouring East, the Possible, springs up. Mutiny of men thou wilt sternly repress; weakness, despondency, thou wilt cheerily encourage: thou wilt swallow down complaint, unreason, weariness, weakness of others and thyself;—how much wilt thou swallow down! There shall be a depth of Silence in thee, deeper than this Sea, which is but ten miles deep: a Silence unsoundable; known to God only. Thou shalt be a great Man. Yes, my World-Soldier, thou of the World Marine-service,—thou wilt have to be *greater* than this tumultuous unmeasured World here round thee is; thou, in thy strong soul, as with wrestler's arms, shalt embrace it, harness it down; and make it bear thee on,—to

Carlyle

new Americas, or whither God wills!

XII: Reward

'Religion,' I said; for, properly speaking, all true Work is Religion: and whatsoever Religion is not Work may go and dwell among the Brahmins, Antinomians, Spinning Dervishes, or where it will; with me it shall have no harbour. Admirable was that of the old Monks, '*Laborare est Orare*, Work is Worship.'

Older than all preached Gospels was this unpreached, inarticulate but ineradicable, forever-enduring Gospel: Work, and therein have well being. Man, son of Earth and of Heaven, lies there not, in the innermost heart of thee, a Spirit of active Method, a Force for work;—and burns like a painfully smouldering fire, giving thee no rest till thou unfold it, till thou write it down in beneficent Facts around thee! What is immethodic, waste, thou shalt make methodic, regulated, arable; obedient and productive to thee. Wheresoever thou findest Disorder, there is thy eternal enemy; attack him swiftly, subdue him; make Order of him, the subject not of Chaos, but of Intelligence, Divinity and Thee! The thistle that grows in thy path, dig it out, that a blade of useful grass, a drop of nourishing milk, may grow there instead. The waste cotton-shrub, gather its waste white down, spin it, weave it; that, in place of idle litter, there may be folded webs, and the naked skin of man be covered.

But above all, where thou findest Ignorance, Stupidity, Brute-mindedness,—yes, there, with or without Church tithes and Shovel-hat, with or without Talfourd-Mahon Copyrights, or were it with mere dungeons and gibbets and crosses, attack it, I say; smite it wisely, unweariedly, and rest not while thou livest and it lives; but smite, smite, in the name of God! The Highest God, as I understand it, does audibly so command thee; still audibly, if thou have ears to hear. He, even He, with his *un*spoken voice, awfuler than any Sinai thunders or syllabled speech of Whirlwinds; for the SILENCE of deep Eternities, of Worlds from beyond the morning-stars, does it not speak to thee? The unborn Ages; the old Graves, with their long-mouldering dust, the very tears that wetted it now all dry,—do not these speak to thee, what ear hath not heard? The deep Death-kingdoms, the Stars in their never-resting courses, all Space and all Time, proclaim it to thee in continual silent admonition. Thou too, if ever man should, shalt work while it is called Today. For the Night cometh, wherein no man can work.

All true Work is sacred; in all true Work, were it but true hand-labour, there is something of divineness. Labour, wide as the Earth, has its summit in Heaven. Sweat of the brow; and up from that to sweat of the brain, sweat of the heart; which includes all Kepler calculations, Newton meditations, all Sciences, all spoken Epics, all acted Heroisms, Martyrdoms,—up to that 'Agony of bloody sweat,' which all men have called divine! O brother, if this is not 'worship' then I say, the more pity for worship; for this is the noblest thing yet discovered under God's sky. Who art thou that corn-plainest of thy life of toil? Complain not. Look up, my wearied brother: see thy fellow Workmen there, in God's Eternity; surviving there, they alone surviving: sacred Band of the Immortals, celestial Bodyguard of the Empire of Mankind. Even in the weak Human Memory they survive so long, as saints, as heroes, as gods; they alone surviving; peopling, they alone, the unmeasured solitudes of Time! To Thee Heaven, though severe, is *not* unkind; Heaven is kind,—as a noble Mother; as that Spartan Mother, saying while she gave her son his shield, "With it, my son, or upon it!" Thou too, shalt return *home* in honour; to thy far-distant Home, in honour; doubt it not,—if in the battle thou keep thy shield! Thou, in the Eternities and deepest Death-kingdoms, art not an alien; thou everywhere art a denizen! Complain not; the very Spartans did not *complain*.

And who art thou that braggest of thy life of Idleness; complacently shewest thy bright gilt equipages; sumptuous cushions; appliances for folding of the hands to mere sleep? Looking up, looking down, around, behind or before, discernest thou, if it be not in Mayfair alone, any *idle* hero, saint, god, or even devil? Not a vestige of one. In the Heavens, in the Earth, in the Waters under the Earth, is none like unto thee. Thou art an original figure in this Creation; a denizen in Mayfair alone, in this extraordinary Century or Half-Century alone! One monster there is in the world: the idle man. What is his 'Religion?' That Nature is a Phantasm, where cunning beggary or thievery may sometimes find good victual. That God is a lie; and that Man and his Life are a lie.—Alas, alas, who of us *is* there that can say, I have worked? The faithfulest of us are unprofitable servants; the faithfulest of us know that best. The faithfulest of us may say, with sad and true old Samuel, "Much of my life has been trifled away!" But he that has, and except 'on public occasions' professes to have, no function but that of going idle in a graceful or graceless manner; and of begetting sons to go idle; and to address Chief Spinners and Diggers, who at least *are* spinning and digging, "Ye scandalous persons who produce too much"—My Corn-Law Friends, on what imaginary still richer Eldorados, and true iron-spikes with law of gravitation, are ye rushing!

As to the Wages of Work there might innumerable things be said; there will and must yet innumerable things be said and spoken, in St. Stephen's and out of St. Stephen's; and gradually not a few things be ascertained and written, on Law-parchment, concerning this very matter: —'Fair day's-wages for a fair day's-work' is the most unrefusable demand! Money-wages 'to the extent of keeping your worker alive that he may work more;' these, unless you mean to dismiss him straightway out of this world, are indispensable alike to the noblest Worker and to the least noble!

One thing only I will say here, in special reference to the former class, the noble and noblest; but throwing light on all the other classes and their arrangements of this difficult matter: The 'wages' of every noble Work do yet lie in Heaven or else Nowhere. Not in Bank-of-England bills, in Owen's Labour-bank, or any the most improved establishment of banking and money-changing, needest thou, heroic soul, present thy account of earnings. Human banks and labour-banks know thee not; or know thee after generations and centuries have passed away, and thou art clean gone from 'rewarding,'—all manner of bank-drafts, shop-tills, and Downing-street Exchequers lying very invisible, so far from thee! Nay, at bottom, dost thou need any reward? Was it thy aim and life-purpose to be filled with good things for thy heroism; to have a life of pomp and ease, and be what men call 'happy' in this world, or in any other world? I answer for thee deliberately, No. The whole spiritual secret of the new epoch lies in this, that thou canst answer for thyself, with thy whole clearness of head and heart, deliberately, No!

My brother, the brave man has to give his Life away. Give it, I advise thee;—thou dost not expect to *sell* thy Life in an adequate manner? What price, for example, would content thee? The just price of thy LIFE to thee,—why, God's entire Creation to thyself, the whole Universe of Space, the whole Eternity of Time, and what they hold: that is the price which would content thee; that, and if thou wilt be candid, nothing short of that! It is thy all; and for it thou wouldst have all. Thou art an unreasonable mortal;—or rather thou art a poor *infinite* mortal, who, in thy narrow clay-prison here, *seemest* so unreasonable! Thou wilt never sell thy Life, or any part of thy Life, in a satisfactory manner. Give it, like a royal heart; let the price be Nothing: thou *hast* then, in a certain sense, got All for it! The heroic man,—and is not every man, God be thanked, a potential hero?—has to do so, in all times and circumstances. In the most heroic age, as in the most unheroic, he will have to say, as Burns said proudly and humbly of his little Scottish Songs, little dewdrops of Celestial Melody in an age when so much was unmelodious: "By Heaven, they shall either be invaluable or of no value; I do not need your guineas for them!" It is an element which should, and must, enter deeply into all settlements of wages here below. They never will be 'satisfactory' otherwise; they cannot, O Mammon Gospel, they never can! Money for my little piece of work 'to the extent that will allow me to keep working;' yes, this,—unless you mean that I shall go my ways *before* the work is all taken out of me: but as to 'wages'—!—

On the whole, we do entirely agree with those old Monks, *Laborare est Orare*. In a thousand senses, from one end of it to the other, true Work *is* Worship. He that works, whatsoever be his work, he bodies forth the form of Things Unseen; a small Poet every Worker is. The idea, were it but of his poor Delf Platter, how much more of his Epic Poem, is as yet 'seen' half-seen, only by himself; to all others it is a thing-unseen, impossible; to Nature herself it is a thing unseen, a thing which never hitherto was;—very 'impossible' for it is as yet a No-thing! The Unseen Powers had need to watch over such a man; he works in and for the Unseen. Alas, if he look to the Seen Powers only, he may as well quit the business; his Nothing will never rightly issue as a Thing, but as a Deceptivity, a Sham-thing,—which it had better not do!

Thy No-thing of an Intended Poem, O Poet who hast looked merely to reviewers, copyrights, booksellers, popularities, behold it has not yet become a Thing; for the truth is not in it! Though printed, hotpressed, reviewed, celebrated, sold to the twentieth edition: what is all that? The Thing, in philosophical uncommercial language, is still a No-thing, mostly semblance, and deception of the sight;—benign Oblivion incessantly gnawing at it, impatient till Chaos to which it belongs do reabsorb it!—

He who takes not counsel of the Unseen and Silent, from him will never come real visibility and speech. Thou must descend to the *Mothers*, to the *Manes* ["spirits of the dead"], and Hercules-like long suffer and labour there, wouldst thou emerge with victory into the sunlight. As in battle and the shock of war,—for is not this a battle?—thou too shalt fear no pain or death, shalt love no ease or life; the voice of festive Lubberlands, the noise of greedy Acheron shall alike lie silent under thy victorious feet. Thy work, like Dante's, shall 'make thee lean for many years.' The world and its wages, its criticisms, counsels, helps, impediments, shall be as a waste ocean-flood; the chaos through which thou art to swim and sail. Not the waste waves and their weedy gulf-streams, shalt thou take for guidance: thy star alone,—'*Se tu segui tua stella!*' ["if you follow your star"] Thy star alone, now clear-beaming over Chaos, nay now by fits gone out, disastrously eclipsed: this only shalt thou strive to follow. O, it is a business, as I fancy, that of weltering your way through Chaos and the murk of Hell! Green-eyed dragons watching you, three-headed Cerberuses,—not without sympathy of their sort! "*Eccovi l' uom ch' è stato all' Inferno*" ["look, there's the man that has been in Hell"] For in fine, as Poet Dryden says, you do walk hand in hand with sheer Madness, all the way,—who is by no means pleasant company! You look fixedly into Madness, and *her* undiscovered, boundless, bottomless Night-empire; that you may extort new Wisdom out of it, as an Eurydice from Tartarus. The higher the Wisdom, the closer was its neighbourhood and kindred with mere Insanity; literally so:—and thou wilt, with a speechless feeling, observe how highest Wisdom, struggling up into this world, has oftentimes carried such tinctures and adhesions of Insanity still cleaving to it hither!

All Works, each in their degree, are a making of Madness sane;—truly enough a religious operation; which cannot be carried on without religion. You have not work otherwise; you have eye-service, greedy grasping of wages, swift and ever swifter manufacture of semblances to get hold of wages. Instead of better felt-hats to cover your head, you have bigger lath-and-plaster hats set travelling the streets on wheels. Instead of heavenly and earthly Guidance for the souls of men, you have 'Black or White Surplice' Controversies, stuffed hair-and-leather Popes;—terrestrial *Law-wards*, Lords and Law-bringers, 'organizing Labour' in these years, by passing Corn-Laws. With all which, alas, this distracted Earth is now full, nigh to bursting. Semblances most smooth to the touch and eye; most accursed nevertheless to body and soul. Semblances, be they of Sham-woven Cloth or of Dilettante Legislation, which are *not* real wool or substance, but Devil's-dust, accursed of God and man! No man has worked, or can work, except religiously; not even the poor day-labourer, the weaver of your coat, the sewer of your shoes. All men, if they work not as in a Great Taskmaster's eye, will work wrong, work unhappily for themselves and you.

Industrial work, still under bondage to Mammon, the rational soul of it not yet awakened, is a tragic spectacle. Men in the rapidest motion and self-motion; restless, with convulsive energy, as if driven by Galvanism, as if possessed by a Devil; tearing asunder mountains,—to no purpose, for Mammonism is always Midas-eared! This is sad, on the face of it. Yet courage: the beneficent Destinies, kind in their sternness, are apprising us that this cannot continue. Labour is not a devil, even while encased in Mammonism; Labour is ever an imprisoned god, writhing unconsciously or consciously to escape out of Mammonism! Plugson of Undershot, like Taillefer of Normandy, wants victory; how much happier will even Plugson be to have a Chivalrous victory than a Chactaw one. The unredeemed ugliness is that of a slothful People. Shew me a People energetically busy; heaving, struggling, all shoulders at the wheel; their heart pulsing, every muscle swelling, with man's energy and will;—I shew you a People of whom great good is already predicable; to whom all manner of good is yet certain, if their energy endure. By very working, they

The Modern Worker

will learn; they have, Antæus-like, their foot on Mother Fact: how can they but learn?

The vulgarest Plugson of a Master-Worker, who can command Workers, and get work out of them, is already a considerable man. Blessed and thrice-blessed symptoms I discern of Master-Workers who are not vulgar men; who are Nobles, and begin to feel that they must act as such: all speed to these, they are England's hope at present! But in this Plugson himself, conscious of almost no nobleness whatever, how much is there! Not without man's faculty, insight, courage, hard energy, is this rugged figure. His words none of the wisest; but his actings cannot be altogether foolish. Think, how were it, stoodest thou suddenly in his shoes! He has to command a thousand men. And not imaginary commanding; no; it is real, incessantly practical. The evil passions of so many men (with the Devil in them, as in all of us) he has to vanquish; by manifold force of speech and of silence, to repress or evade. What a force of silence, to say nothing of the others, is in Plugson! For these his thousand men he has to provide raw-material, machinery, arrangement, house-room; and ever at the week's end, wages by due sale. No Civil-List, or Goulburn-Baring Budget has he to fall back upon, for paying of his regiment; he has to pick his supplies from the confused face of the whole Earth and Contemporaneous History, by his dexterity alone. There will be dry eyes if he fail to do it!—He exclaims, at present, 'black in the face,' near strangled with Dilettante Legislation: "Let me have elbow-room, throat-room, and I will not fail! No, I will spin yet, and conquer like a giant; what 'sinews of war' lie in me, untold resources towards the Conquest of this Planet, if instead of hanging me, you husband them, and help me!"—My indomitable friend, it is *true*; and thou shalt and must be helped.

This is not a man I would kill and strangle by Corn-Laws, even if I could! No, I would fling my Corn-Laws and Shot-belts to the Devil; and try to help this man. I would teach him, by noble precept and law-precept, by noble example most of all, that Mammonism was not the essence of his or of my station in God's Universe; but the adscititious excrescence of it; the gross, terrene, godless embodiment of it; which would have to become, more or less, a godlike one. By noble *real* legislation, by true *noble's*-work, by unwearied, valiant, and were it wageless effort, in my Parliament and in my

Parish, I would aid, constrain, encourage him to effect more or less this blessed change. I should know that it would have to be effected; that unless it were in some measure effected, he and I and all of us, I first and soonest of all, were doomed to perdition!—Effected it will be; unless it were a Demon that made this Universe; which I, for my own part, do at no moment, under no form, in the least believe.

May it please your Serene Highnesses, your Majesties, Lordships and Law-wardships, the proper Epic of this world is not now 'Arms and the Man;' how much less, 'Shirt-frills and the Man:' no, it is now 'Tools and the Man:' that, henceforth to all time is now our Epic; and you, first of all others, I think, were wise to take note of that!

XIII: Democracy

IF the Serene Highnesses and Majesties do not take note of that, then, as I perceive, *that* will take note of itself! The time for levity, insincerity, and idle babble and play-acting, in all kinds, is gone by; it is a serious, grave time. Old long-vexed questions, not yet solved in logical words or parliamentary laws, are fast solving themselves in facts, somewhat unblessed to behold! This largest of questions, this question of Work and Wages, which ought, had we heeded Heaven's voice to have begun two generations ago or more, cannot be delayed longer without hearing Earth's voice. 'Labour' will verily need to be somewhat 'organised,' as they say,—God knows with what difficulty. Man will actually need to have his debts and earnings a little better paid by man; which, let Parliaments speak of them or be silent of them, are eternally his due from man, and cannot, without penalty and at length not without death-penalty, be withheld. How much ought to cease among us straightway; how much ought to begin straightway, while the hours yet are!

Truly they are strange results to which this of leaving all to 'Cash;' of quietly shutting up the God's Temple, and gradually opening wide-open the Mammon's Temple, with 'Laissez-faire, and Everyman for himself,'—have led us in these days! We have Upper, speaking Classes, who indeed do 'speak' as never man spake before; the withered flimsiness, the godless baseness and barrenness of whose Speech might of itself indicate what kind of Doing and practical Governing went on under it! For Speech is the gaseous element out of which most kinds of Practice and Performance, especially all kinds of moral Performance, condense themselves, and take shape; as the one is, so will the other be. Descending, accordingly, into the Dumb Class in its Stockport Cellars and Poor-Law Bastilles, have we not to announce that they also are hitherto unexampled in the History of Adam's Posterity?

Life was never a May-game for men: in all times the lot of the dumb millions born to toil was defaced with manifold sufferings, injustices, heavy burdens, avoidable and unavoidable; not play at all, but hard work that made the sinews sore, and the heart sore. As bond-slaves, *villani, bordarii, sochemanni*, nay indeed as dukes, earls and kings, men were oftentimes made weary of their life; and had to say, in the sweat of their brow and of their soul, Behold it is not sport, it is grim earnest, and our back can bear no more! Who knows not what massacrings and harryings there have been; grinding, long-continuing, unbearable injustices,—till the heart had to rise in madness, and some "*Eu Sachsen, nimith euer sachses*, You Saxons, out with your gully-knives then!" You Saxons, some 'arrestment,' partial 'arrestment of the Knaves and Dastards' has become indispensable!—The page of Dryasdust is heavy with such details.

And yet I will venture to believe that in no time, since the beginnings of Society, was the lot of those same dumb millions of toilers so entirely unbearable as it is even in the days now passing over us. It is not to die, or even to die of hunger, that makes a man wretched; many men have died; all men must die,—the last exit of us all is in a Fire-Chariot of Pain. But it is to live miserable we know not why; to work sore and yet gain nothing; to be heart-worn, weary, yet isolated, unrelated, girt in with a cold universal Laissez-faire: it is to die slowly all our life long, imprisoned in a deaf, dead, Infinite Injustice, as in the accursed iron belly of a Phalaris' Bull! This is and remains forever intolerable to all men whom God has made. Do we wonder at French Revolutions, Chartisms, Revolts of Three Days? The times, if we will consider them, are really unexampled.

Never before did I hear of an Irish Widow reduced to 'prove her sisterhood by dying of typhus-fever and infecting seventeen persons,'—saying in such undeniable way, "You *see*, I was your sister!" Sisterhood, brotherhood was often forgotten: but not till the rise of these ultimate Mammon and Shot-belt Gospels, did I ever see it so expressly denied. If no pious Lord or *Law-ward* would remember it, always some pious Lady ('*Hlaf-dig*' Benefactress, '*Loaf-giveress*,' they say she is,—blessings on her beautiful heart!) was there, with mild mother-voice and hand, to remember it; some pious thoughtful *Elder*, what we now call 'Prester,' *Presbyter* or 'Priest,' was there to put all men in mind of it, in the name of the God who had made all.

Not even in Black Dahomey was it ever, I think, forgotten to the typhus-fever length. Mungo Park, resourceless, had sunk down to die under the Negro Village-Tree, a horrible White object in the eyes of all. But in the poor Black Woman, and her daughter who stood aghast at him, whose earthly wealth and funded capital consisted of one small calabash of rice, there lived a heart richer than '*Laissez-faire*:' they, with a royal munificence, boiled their rice for him; they sang all night to him, spinning assiduous on their cotton distaffs, as he lay to sleep: "Let us pity the poor white man; no mother has he to fetch him milk, no sister to grind him corn!" Thou poor black Noble One,—thou *Lady* too: did not a God make thee too; was there not in thee too something of a God!—

Gurth born thrall of Cedric the Saxon has been greatly pitied by Dryasdust and others. Gurth with the brass collar round his neck, tending Cedric's pigs in the glades of the wood, is not what I call an exemplar of human felicity: but Gurth, with the sky above him, with the free air and tinted boscage and umbrage round him, and in him at least the certainty of supper and social lodging when he came home; Gurth to me seems happy, in comparison with many a Lancashire and Buckinghamshire man, of these days, not born thrall of anybody! Gurth's brass collar did not gall him: Cedric *deserved* to be his Master. The pigs were Cedric's, but Gurth too would get his parings of them. Gurth had the inexpressible satisfaction of feeling himself related indissolubly, though in a rude brass-collar way, to his fellow-mortals in this Earth. He had superiors, inferiors, equals.—Gurth is now 'emancipated' long since; has what we call 'Liberty.' Liberty, I am told, is a Divine thing. Liberty when it becomes the 'Liberty to die by starvation' is not so divine!

Liberty? The true liberty of a man you would say, consisted in his finding out, or being forced to find out the right path, and to walk thereon. To learn or to be taught, what work he actually was able for; and then by permission, persuasion, and even compulsion, to set about doing of the same! That is his true blessedness, honour, 'liberty' and maximum of well being: if liberty be not that, I for one have small care about liberty. You do not allow a palpable madman to leap over precipices; you violate his liberty, you that are wise; and keep him, were it in straight-waistcoats, away from the precipices! Every stupid, every cowardly and foolish man is but a less palpable madman: his true liberty were that a wiser man, that any and every wiser man, could, by brass collars, or in whatever milder or sharper way, lay hold of him when he was going wrong, and order and compel him to go a little righter. O if thou really art my *Senior*, Seigneur, my *Elder*, Presbyter or Priest,—if thou art in very deed my *Wiser*, may a beneficent instinct lead and impel thee to 'conquer' me, to command me! If thou do know better than I what is good and right, I conjure you in the name of God, force me to do it; were it by never such brass collars, whips and handcuffs, leave me not to walk over precipices! That I have been called, by all the Newspapers, a 'free man' will avail me little, if my pilgrimage have ended in death and wreck. O that the Newspapers had called me slave, coward, fool, or what it pleased their sweet voices to name me, and I had attained not death, but life!—Liberty requires new definitions.

A conscious abhorrence and intolerance of Folly, of Baseness, Stupidity, Poltroonery and all that brood of things, dwells deep in some men: still deeper in others and *un*conscious abhorrence and intolerance, clothed moreover by the beneficent Supreme Powers in what stout appetites, energies, egoisms so-called, are suitable to it;—these latter are your Conquerors, Romans, Normans, Russians, Indo-English; Founders of what we call Aristocracies. Which indeed have they not the most 'divine right' to found;—being themselves very truly Αριστοι, Bravest, Best; and conquering generally a confused rabble of Worst, or at lowest, clearly enough, of Worse? I think their divine right, tried with affirmatory verdict, in the greatest Law-Court known to me, was good! A class of men who are dreadfully exclaimed against by Dryasdust; of whom nevertheless beneficent Nature has oftentimes had need; and may, alas, again have need.

When, across the hundredfold poor scepticisms, trivialisms, and constitutional cobwebberies of Dryasdust, you catch any glimpse of a William the Conqueror, a Tancred of Hauteville or such like,—do you not discern veritably some rude outline of a true God-made King; whom not the Champion of England cased in tin, but all Nature and the Universe

The Modern Worker

were calling to the throne? It is absolutely necessary that he get thither. Nature does not mean her poor Saxon children to perish, of obesity, stupor or other malady, as yet: a stern Ruler and Line of Rulers therefore is called in,—a stern but most beneficent *Perpetual House-Surgeon* is by Nature herself called in, and even the appropriate *fees* are provided for him! Dryasdust talks lamentably about Hereward and the Fen Counties; fate of Earl Waltheof; Yorkshire and the North reduced to ashes; all which is undoubtedly lamentable. But even Dryasdust apprises me of one fact: 'A child, in this William's reign, might have carried a purse of gold from end to end of England.' My erudite friend, it is a fact which outweighs a thousand! Sweep away thy constitutional, sentimental and other cobwebberies; look eye to eye, if thou still have any eye, in the face of this big burly William Bastard: thou wilt see a fellow of most flashing discernment, of most strong lion-heart;—in whom, as it were, within a frame of oak and iron, the gods have planted the soul of 'a man of genius!' Dost thou call that nothing? I call it an immense thing!—Rage enough was in this Willelmus Conquestor, rage enough for his occasions;—and yet the essential element of him, as of all such men, is not scorching *fire*, but shining illuminative *light*. Fire and light are strangely interchangeable; nay, at bottom, I have found them different forms of the same most godlike 'elementary substance' in our world: a thing worth stating in these days. The essential element of this Conquestor is, first of all, the most sun-eyed perception of what is really what on this God's-Earth;—which, thou wilt find, does mean at bottom 'Justice,' and 'Virtues' not a few: *Conformity* to what the Maker has been good to make; that, I suppose, will mean Justice and a Virtue or two?—

Dost thou think Willelmus Conquestor would have tolerated ten years' jargon, on the propriety of killing Cotton-manufactures by partridge Corn-Laws? I fancy, this was not the man to knock out of his night's-rest with nothing but a noisy bedlamism in your mouth! "Assist us still better to bush the partridges; strangle Plugson who spins the shirts?"—"*Par la Splendeur de Dieu!*" ["by the splendour of God"]——Dost thou think Willelmus Conquestor, in this new time, with Steamengine Captains of Industry on one hand of him, and Joe-Manton Captains of Idleness on the other, would have doubted which was really the Best; which did deserve strangling, and which not?

I have a certain indestructible regard for Willelmus Conquestor. A resident House-Surgeon, provided by Nature for her beloved English People, and even furnished with the requisite fees as I said; for he by no means felt himself doing Nature's work, this Willelmus, but his own work exclusively! And his own work withal it was; informed '*par la Splendeur de Dieu.*'—I say, it is necessary to get the work out of such a man, however harsh that be! When a world, not yet doomed for death, is rushing down to ever-deeper Baseness and Confusion, it is a dire necessity of Nature's to bring in her ARISTOCRACIES, her BEST, even by forcible methods. When their descendants or representatives cease entirely to *be* the Best, Nature's poor world will very soon rush down again to Baseness; and it becomes a dire necessity of Nature's to cast them out. Hence French Revolutions, Five-point Charters, Democracies, and a mournful list of *Etceteras*, in these our afflicted times.

To what extent Democracy has now reached, how it advances irresistible with ominous, ever-increasing speed, he that will open his eyes on any province of human affairs may discern. Democracy is everywhere the inexorable demand of these ages, swiftly fulfilling itself. From the thunder of Napoleon battles, to the jabbering of Open-vestry in St. Mary Axe, all things announce Democracy. A distinguished man, whom some of my readers will hear again with pleasure, thus writes to me what in these days he notes from the Wahngasse of Weissnichtwo, where our London fashions seem to be in full vogue. Let us hear the Herr Teufelsdröckh again, were it but the smallest word!

'Democracy, which means despair of finding any Heroes to govern you, and contented putting up with the want of them,—alas, thou too, *mein Lieber* ["my dear"], seest well how close it is of kin to *Atheism*, and other sad *Isms*: he who discovers no God whatever, how shall he discover Heroes, the visible Temples of God?—Strange enough meanwhile it is, to observe with what thoughtlessness, here in our rigidly Conservative Country, men rush into Democracy with full cry. Beyond doubt, his Excellenz the Titular Herr Ritter Kauderwälsch von Pferdefuss-Quacksalber, he our distinguished Conservative Premier himself, and all but the thicker-headed of his Party, discern Democracy to be inevitable as death, and are even desperate of delaying it much!

'You cannot walk the streets without beholding Democracy announce itself: the very Tailor has become, if not properly Sansculottic, which to him would be ruinous, yet a Tailor unconsciously symbolising, and prophesying with his scissors, the reign of Equality. What now is our fashionable coat? A thing of superfinest texture, of deeply meditated cut; with Malines-lace cuffs; quilted with gold; so that a man can carry without difficulty an estate of land on his back? *Keinesiwegs* ["not at all"], By no manner of means! The Sumptuary Laws have fallen into such a state of desuetude as was never before seen. Our fashionable coat is an amphibium between barnsack and drayman's doublet. The cloth of it is studiously coarse; the colour a speckled soot-black or rust-brown grey;—the nearest approach to a Peasant's. And for shape, thou shouldst see it! The last consummation of the year now passing over us is definable as Three Bags: a big bag for the body, two small bags for the arms, and by way of collar a hem! The first Antique Cheruscan who, of felt-cloth or bear's-hide, with bone or metal needle, set about making himself a coat, before Tailors had yet awakened out of Nothing,—did not he make it even so? A loose wide poke for body, with two holes to let out the arms; this was his original coat: to which holes it was soon visible that two small loose pokes, or sleeves, easily appended, would be an improvement.

'Thus has the Tailor art, so to speak, overset itself, like most other things; changed its centre-of-gravity; whirled suddenly over from zenith to nadir. Your Stulz, with huge somerset, vaults from his high shopboard down to the depths of primal savagery,—carrying much along with him! For I will invite thee to reflect that the Tailor, as topmost ultimate froth of Human Society, is indeed swift-passing, evanescent, slippery to decipher; yet significant of much, nay of all. Topmost evanescent froth, he is churned up from the very lees, and from all intermediate regions of the liquor. The general outcome he, visible to the eye, of what men aimed to do, and were obliged and enabled to do, in this one public department of symbolising themselves to each other by covering of their skins. A smack of all Human Life lies in the Tailor: its wild struggles towards beauty, dignity, freedom, victory; and how, hemmed in by Sedan and Huddersfield, by Nescience, Dulness, Prurience, and other sad necessities and laws of Nature, it has attained just to this: Grey savagery of Three Sacks with a hem!

'When the very Tailor verges toward Sansculottism, is it not ominous? The last Divinity of poor mankind dethroning himself; sinking *his* taper too, flame downmost, like the Genius of Sleep or of Death; admonitory that Tailor-time shall be no more!—For, little as one could advise Sumptuary Laws at the present epoch, yet nothing is clearer than that where ranks do actually exist, strict division of costumes will also be enforced; that if we ever have a new Hierarchy and Aristocracy, acknowledged veritably as such, for which I daily pray Heaven, the Tailor will reawaken; and be, by volunteering and appointment, consciously and unconsciously, a safeguard of that same'—Certain further observations, from the same invaluable pen, on our never-ending changes of mode, our 'perpetual nomadic and even ape-like appetite for change and mere change' in all the equipments of our existence, and the 'fatal revolutionary character' thereby manifested, we suppress for the present. It may be admitted that Democracy, in all meanings of the word, is in full career; irresistible by any Ritter Kauderwalsch or other Son of Adam, as times go. 'Liberty' is a thing men are determined to have.

But truly, as I have to remark in the meanwhile, 'the liberty of not being oppressed by your fellow man' is an indispensable, yet one of the most insignificant fractional parts of Human Liberty. No man oppresses thee, can bid thee fetch or carry, come or go, without reason shown. True; from all men thou art emancipated: but from Thyself and from the Devil—? No man, wiser, unwiser, can make thee come or go: but thy own futilities, bewilderments, thy false appetites for Money, Windsor Georges and such like? No man oppresses thee, O free and independent Franchiser: but does not this stupid Porter-pot oppress thee? No Son of Adam can bid thee come or go; but this absurd Pot of Heavy wet, this can and does! Thou art the thrall not of Cedric the Saxon, but of thy own brutal appetites, and this scoured dish of liquor. And thou pratest of thy 'liberty?' Thou entire blockhead!

Heavy-wet and gin: alas, these are not the only kinds of thraldom. Thou who walkest in a vain shew, looking out with ornamental dilettante sniff, and serene supremacy, at all Life and all Death; and amblest jauntily; perking up thy poor talk into crochets, thy poor conduct into fatuous somnambulisms;—and *art* as an 'enchanted Ape' under God's sky, where thou mightest have been a man, had proper Schoolmasters and Conquerors, and Constables with cat-o'-nine tails, been vouchsafed thee; dost thou call that 'liberty?' Or your unreposing Mammon-worshipper, again, driven, as if by Galvanisms, by Devils and Fixed-Ideas, who rises early and sits late, chasing the impossible; straining every faculty. To 'fill himself with the east wind,'—how merciful were it, could you, by mild persuasion or by the severest tyranny so-called, check him in his mad path, and turn him into a wiser one! All painful tyranny, in that case again, were but mild 'surgery;' the pain of it cheap, as health and life, instead of galvanism and fixed-idea, are cheap at any price.

Sure enough, of all paths a man could strike into, there *is*, at any given moment, a *best path* for every man; a thing which, here and now, it were of all things *wisest* for him to do;— which could he be but led or driven to do, he were then doing 'like a man,' as we phrase it; all men and gods agreeing with him, the whole Universe virtually exclaiming Well-done to him! His success, in such case, were complete; his felicity a maximum. This path, to find this path and walk in it, is the one thing needful for him. Whatsoever forwards him in that, let it come to him even in the shape of blows and spurnings, is liberty: whatsoever hinders him, were it wardmotes, open-vestries, pollbooths tremendous cheers, rivers of heavy-wet, is slavery.

The notion that a man's liberty consists in giving his vote at election-hustings, and saying, "Behold now I too have my twenty-thousandth part of a Talker in our National Palaver; will not all the gods be good to me?"—is one of the pleasantest! Nature nevertheless is kind at present; and puts it into the heads of many, almost of all. The liberty especially which has to purchase itself by social isolation, and each man standing separate from the other, having 'no business with him' but a cash-account: this is such a liberty as the Earth seldom saw;—as the Earth will not long put up with, recommend it how you may. This liberty turns out, before it have long continued in action, with all men flinging up their caps round it, to be, for the Working Millions a liberty to die by want of food; for the Idle Thousands and Units, alas, a still more fatal liberty to live in want of work; to have no earnest duty to do in this God's-World any more. What becomes of a man in such predicament? Earth's Laws are silent; and Heaven's speak in a voice which is not heard. No work, and the ineradicable need of work, give rise to new very wondrous life-philosophies, new very wondrous life-practices! Dilettantism, Pococurantism, Beau-Brummelism, with perhaps an occasional, half-mad, protesting burst of Byronism, establish themselves: at the end of a certain period, if you go back to 'the Dead Sea,' there is, say our Moslem friends, a very strange 'Sabbath-day' transacting itself there!—Brethren, we know but imperfectly yet, after ages of Constitutional Government, what Liberty and Slavery are.

Democracy, the chase of Liberty in that direction, shall go its full course; unrestrainable by him of Pferdefuss-Quack-salber, or any of *his* household. The Toiling Millions of Mankind, in most vital need and passionate instinctive desire of Guidance, shall cast away False-Guidance; and hope, for an hour, that No-Guidance will suffice them: but it can be for an hour only. The smallest item of human Slavery is the oppression of man by his Mock-Superiors; the palpablest, but I say at bottom the smallest. Let him shake off such oppression, trample it indignantly under his feet; I blame him not, I pity and commend him. But oppression by your Mock-Superiors well shaken off, the grand problem yet remains to solve: That of finding government by your Real-Superiors! Alas, how shall we ever learn the solution of that, benighted, bewildered, sniffing, sneering, godforgetting unfortunates as we are? It is a work for centuries; to be taught us by tribulations, confusions, insurrections, obstructions; who knows if not by conflagration and despair! It is a lesson inclusive of all other lessons; the hardest of all lessons to learn.

One thing I do know: Those Apes, chattering on the branches by the Dead Sea, never got it learned; but chatter there to this day. To them no Moses need come a second time; a thousand Moseses would be but so many painted Phantasms, interesting Fellow-Apes of new strange aspect,—whom they would 'invite to dinner,' be glad to meet with in lion-soirées. To them the voice of Prophecy, of heavenly monition, is quite ended. They chatter there, all Heaven shut to them, to the end of the world. The unfortunates! O, what is dying of hunger, with honest tools in your hand, with a manful purpose in your heart, and much real labour lying round you done in comparison? You honestly quit your tools; quit a most muddy, confused coil of sore work, short rations, of sorrows, dispiritments and contradictions, having now honestly done with it all;—and await, not entirely in a distracted manner, what the Supreme Powers, and the Silences and the Eternities may have to say to you.

A second thing I know: This lesson will have to be learned,— under penalties! England will either learn it, or England also will cease to exist among Nations. England will either learn to reverence its Heroes, and discriminate them from its Sham-Heroes and Valets and gaslighted Histrios; and to prize them as the audible God's-voice, amid all inane jargons and temporary market-cries, and say to them with heart-loyalty, "Be ye King and Priest, and Gospel and Guidance for us:" or else England will continue to worship new and ever-new forms of Quackhood,—and so, with what resiliences and reboundings matters little, go down to the Father of Quacks! Can I dread such things of England? Wretched, thick-eyed, gross-hearted mortals, why will ye worship lies, and 'Stuffed Clothes-suits, created by the ninth-parts of men!' It is not your purses that suffer; your farm-rents, your commerces, your mill-revenues, loud as ye lament over these; no, it is not these alone, but a far deeper than these: it is your souls that lie dead, crushed down under despicable Nightmares, Atheisms, Brain-fumes; and are not souls at all, but mere succedanea for *salt* to keep your bodies and their appetites from putrefying! Your cotton-spinning and thrice-miraculous mechanism, what is this too, by itself, but a larger kind of Animalism? Spiders can spin, Beavers can build and shew contrivance; the Ant lays up accumulation of capital, and has, for aught I know, a Bank of Antland. If there is no soul in man higher than all that, did it reach to sailing on the cloud-rack and spinning sea-sand; then I say, man is but an animal, a more cunning kind of brute: he has no soul, but only a succedaneum for salt. Whereupon, seeing himself to be truly of the beasts that perish, he ought to admit it, I think;—and also straightway universally to kill himself; and so, in a manlike manner, at least, *end* and wave these brute-worlds *his* dignified farewell!—

XIV: Sir Jabesh Windbag

OLIVER CROMWELL, whose body they hung on their Tyburn Gallows because he had found the Christian Religion inexecutable in this country, remains to me by far the remarkablest Governor we have had here for the last five centuries or so. For the last five centuries, there has been no Governor among us with anything like similar talent; and for the last two centuries, no Governor, we may say, with the possibility of similar talent,—with an idea in the heart of him capable of inspiring similar talent, capable of coexisting therewith. When you consider that Oliver believed in a God, the difference between Oliver's position and that of any subsequent Governor of this Country becomes, the more you reflect on it, the more immeasurable!

Oliver, no volunteer in Public Life, but plainly a ballotted soldier strictly ordered thither, enters upon Public Life; comports himself there like a man who carried his own life in his hand; like a man whose Great Commander's eye was always on him. Not without results. Oliver, well advanced in years, finds now, by Destiny and his own Deservings, or as he himself better phrased it, by wondrous successive 'Births of Providence,' the Government of England put into his hands. In senate-house and battle-field, in counsel and in action, in private and in public, this man has proved himself a man: England and the voice of God, through waste awful whirlwinds and environments, speaking to his great heart, summon him to assert formally, in the way of solemn Public Fact and as a new piece of English Law, what informally and by Nature's eternal Law needed no asserting, That he, Oliver, was the Ablest-Man of England, the King of England; that he, Oliver, would undertake governing England. His way of making the same 'assertion' the one way he had of making it, has given rise to immense criticism: but the assertion itself in what way soever 'made,' is it not somewhat of a solemn one, somewhat of a tremendous one!

And now do but contrast this Oliver with my right honourable friend Sir Jabesh Windbag, Mr. Facing-both-ways, Viscount Mealymouth, Earl of Windlestraw, or what other Cagliostro, Cagliostrino, Cagliostraccio, the course of Fortune and Parliamentary Majorities has constitutionally guided to that dignity, any time during these last sorrowful hundred-and-fifty years! Windbag, weak in the faith of a God, which he believes only at Church on Sundays, if even then; strong only in the faith that Paragraphs and Plausibilities bring votes; that force of Public Opinion as he calls it, is the primal Necessity of Things, and highest God we have:—Wind-bag, if we will consider him, has a problem set before him which may be ranged in the impossible class. He is a Columbus minded to sail to the indistinct country of NOWHERE, to the indistinct country of WHITHERWARD, by the *friendship* of those same waste-tumbling Water-Alps and howling waltz of All the Winds; not by conquest of them and in spite of them, but by friendship of them, when once *they* have made up their mind! He is the most original Columbus I ever saw. Nay, his problem is not an impossible one: he will infallibly *arrive* at that same country of NOWHERE; his indistinct Whitherward will be a *Thither*-ward! In the Ocean Abysses and Locker of Davy Jones, there certainly enough do he and *his* ship's company, and all their cargo and navigatings, at last find lodgement.

Oliver knew that his America lay THERE, Westward Ho: —and it was not entirely by *friendship* of the Water-Alps, and yeasty insane Froth-Oceans, that he meant to get thither! He sailed accordingly; had compass-card, and Rules of Navigation,—older and greater than these Froth-Oceans, old as the Eternal God! Or again, do but think of this. Windbag in these his probable five years of office has to prosper and get Paragraphs: the Paragraphs of these five years must be his salvation, or he is a lost man; redemption nowhere in the Worlds or in the Times discoverable for him. Oliver too would like his Paragraphs; successes, popularities in these five years are not undesirable to him: but mark, I say, this enormous circumstance: *after* these five years are gone and done, comes an Eternity for Oliver! Oliver has to appear before the Most High Judge: the utmost flow of Paragraphs, the utmost ebb of them, is now, in strictest arithmetic, verily no matter at all; its exact value *zero*; an account altogether erased! Enormous;—which a man, in these days, hardly fancies with an effort! Oliver's Paragraphs are all done, his battles, division-lists, successes all summed: and now in that awful unerring Court of Review, the real question first rises, Whether he has succeeded at all; whether he has not been defeated miserably forevermore? Let him come with worldwide *Io-Pæans*, these avail him not. Let him come covered over with the world's execrations, gashed with ignominious death-wounds, the gallows-rope about his neck: what avails that? The word is, Come thou brave and faithful; the word is, Depart thou quack and accursed!

O Windbag, my right honourable friend, in very truth I pity thee. I say, these Paragraphs, and low or loud votings of thy poor fellow-blockheads of mankind, will never guide thee in any enterprise at all. Govern a country on such guidance? Thou canst not make a pair of shoes, sell a penny-worth of tape, on such. No, thy shoes are vamped up falsely to meet the market; behold, the leather only *seemed* to be tanned; thy shoes melt under me to rubbishy pulp, and are not veritable mud-defying shoes, but plausible vendible similitudes of shoes,—thou unfortunate, and I! O my right honourable friend, when the Paragraphs flowed in, who was like Sir Jabesh? On the swelling tide he mounted; higher, higher, triumphant, heaven-high. But the Paragraphs again ebbed out, as unwise Paragraphs needs must: Sir Jabesh lies stranded, sunk and forever sinking in ignominious ooze; the Mud-nymphs, and ever-deepening bottomless Oblivion, his portion to eternal time. 'Posterity?' Thou appealest to Posterity, thou? My right honourable friend, what will Posterity do for thee! The voting of Posterity, were it continued through centuries in thy favour, will be quite inaudible, extra-forensic, without any effect whatever. Posterity can do simply nothing for a man; nor even seem to do much, if the man be not brainsick. Besides, to tell thee truth, the bets are a thousand to one, Posterity will not hear of thee, my right honourable friend! Posterity, I have found, has generally his own Windbags sufficiently trumpeted in all marketplaces, and no leisure to attend to ours. Posterity which has made of Norse Odin a similitude, and of Norman William a brute monster, what will or can it make of English Jabesh? O Heavens, 'Posterity!'—

"These poor persecuted Scotch Covenanters," said I to my inquiring Frenchman, in such stinted French as stood at command, "*Ils s'en appelaient à*" ["they appealed to"]—"*A la Postérité,*" ["to posterity"] interrupted he, helping me out. —"*Ah, Monsieur, non, mille fois non!*" ["Ah sir, no, a thousand times no"] "They appealed to the Eternal God; not to Posterity at all! *C'était different.*" ["it was different"]

XV: Morrison Again

Nevertheless, O advanced Liberal, one cannot promise thee any 'New Religion,' for some time; to say truth, I do not think we have the smallest chance of any! Will the candid reader, by way of closing this Book Third, listen to a few transient remarks on that subject?

Candid readers have not lately met with any man who had less notion to interfere with their Thirty-Nine, or other Church-Articles; wherewith, very helplessly, as is like, they may have struggled to form for themselves some not inconceivable hypothesis about this Universe, and their own Existence there. Superstition, my friend, is far from me; Fanaticism, for any *Fanum* ["shrine"] likely to arise soon on this Earth, is far. A man's Church-Articles are surely articles of price to him; and in these times one has to be tolerent of many strange 'Articles,' and of many still stranger 'No-articles,' which go about placarding themselves in a very distracted manner,—the numerous long placard-poles, and questionable infirm paste-pots, interfering with one's peaceable thoroughfare sometimes!

Fancy a man, moreover, recommending his fellow-men to believe in God, that so Chartism might abate, and the Manchester Operatives be got to spin peaceably! The idea is more distracted than any placard-pole seen hitherto in a public thoroughfare of men! My friend, if thou ever do come to believe in God, thou wilt find all Chartism, Manchester riot, Parliamentary incompetence, Ministries of Windbag, and the wildest Social Dissolutions, and the burning up of this entire Planet, a most small matter in comparison. Brother, this Planet, I find, is but an inconsiderable sandgrain in the continents of Being: this Planet's poor temporary interests, thy interests and my interests there, when I looked fixedly into that eternal Light-Sea and Flame-Sea with *its* eternal interests, dwindle literally into Nothing; my speech of it is—silence for the while. I will as soon think of making Galaxies and Star-Systems to guide little herring-vessels by, as of preaching Religion that the Constable may continue possible. O my Advanced-Liberal friend, this new second progress, of proceeding 'to invent God,' is a very strange one! Jacobinism unfolded into Saint-Simonism bodes innumerable blessed things; but the thing itself might draw tears from a Stoic!—As for me, some twelve or thirteen New Religions, heavy Packets, most of them unfranked, having arrived here from various parts of the world, in a space of six calendar months, I have instructed my invaluable friend the Stamped Postman to introduce no more of them, if the charge exceed one penny.

Henry of Essex, duelling in that Thames Island, 'near to Reading Abbey,' had a religion. But was it in virtue of his seeing armed Phantasms of St. Edmund 'on the rim of the horizon,' looking minatory on him? Had that, intrinsically, anything to do with his religion at all? Henry of Essex's religion was the Inner Light or Moral Conscience of his own soul; such as is vouchsafed still to all souls of men;—which Inner Light shone here 'through such intellectual and other media' as there were; producing 'Phantasms,' Kircherean Visual-Spectra, according to circumstances! It is so with all men. The clearer my Inner Light may shine, through the less turbid media; the *fewer* Phantasms it may produce,—the gladder surely shall I be, and not the sorrier! Hast thou reflected, O serious reader, Advanced-Liberal or other, that the one end, essence, use of all religion past, present and to come, was this only: To keep that same Moral Conscience or Inner Light of ours alive and shining;—which certainly the 'Phantasms' and the 'turbid media' were not essential for! All religion was here to remind us, better or worse, of what we already know better or worse, of the quite *infinite* difference there is between a Good man and a Bad; to bid us love infinitely the one, abhor and avoid infinitely the other,—strive infinitely to *be* the one, and not to be the other. 'All religion issues in due Practical Hero-worship.' He that has a soul unasphyxied will never want a religion; he that has a soul asphyxied, reduced to a succedaneum for salt, will never find any religion, though you rose from the dead to preach him one.

But indeed, when men and reformers ask for 'a religion' it is analogous to their asking, 'What would you have us to do?' and such like. They fancy that their religion too shall be a kind of Morrison's Pill, which they have only to swallow once, and all will be well. Resolutely once gulp down your Religion, your Morrison's Pill, you have it all plain sailing now: you can follow your affairs, your no-affairs, go along money hunting, pleasure-hunting, dilettanteing, dangling, and miming and chattering like a Dead-Sea Ape: your Morrison will do your business for you. Men's notions are very strange!—Brother, I say there is not, was not, nor will ever be, in the wide circle of Nature, any Pill or Religion of that character. Man cannot afford thee such; for the very gods it is impossible. I advise thee to renounce Morrison; once for all, quit hope of the Universal Pill. For body, for soul, for individual or society, there has not any such article been made. *Non extat* ["it does not exist"]. In Created Nature it is not, was not, will not be. In the void imbroglios of Chaos only, and realms of Bedlam, does some shadow of it hover, to bewilder and bemock the poor inhabitants *there*.

Rituals, Liturgies, Creeds, Hierarchies: all this is not religion; all this, were it dead as Odinism, as Fetishism, does not kill religion at all! It is Stupidity alone, with never so many rituals, that kills religion. Is not this still a world? Spinning Cotton under Arkwright and Adam Smith; founding Cities by the Fountain of Juturna, on the Janiculum Mount; tilling Canaan under Prophet Samuel and Psalmist David, man is ever man; the missionary of Unseen Powers; and great and victorious, while he continues true to his mission; mean, miserable, foiled, and at last annihilated and trodden out of sight and memory, when he proves untrue. Brother, thou art a Man, I think; thou art not a mere building Beaver, or two-legged Cotton-Spider; thou hast verily a Soul in thee, asphyxied or otherwise! Sooty Manchester,—it too is built on the infinite Abysses; overspanned by the skyey Firmaments; and there is birth in it, and death in it;—and it is every whit as wonderful, as fearful, unimaginable, as the oldest Salem or Prophetic City. Go or stand, in what time, in what place we will, are there not Immensities, Eternities over us, around us, in us:

'Solemn before us,
Veiled, the dark Portal,

> Goal of all mortal;—
> Stars silent rest o'er us,
> Graves under us silent!'

Between *these* two great Silences, the hum of all our spinning cylinders, Trades-Unions, Anti-Corn-Law Leagues and Carlton Clubs goes on. Stupidity itself ought to pause a little, and consider that. I tell thee, through all thy Ledgers, Supply-and-demand Philosophies, and daily most modern melancholy Business and Cant, there does shine the presence of a Primeval Unspeakable; and thou wert wise to recognise, not with lips only, that same!

The Maker's Laws, whether they are promulgated in Sinai Thunder, to the ear or imagination, or quite otherwise promulgated, are the Laws of God; transcendent, everlasting, imperatively demanding obedience from all men. This, without any thunder, or with never so much thunder, thou, if there be any soul left in thee, canst know of a truth. The Universe, I say, is made by Law; the great Soul of the World is just and not unjust. Look thou, if thou have eyes or soul left, into this great shoreless Incomprehensible; in the heart of its tumultuous Appearances, Embroilments, and mad Time-vortexes, is there not, silent, eternal, an All-just, an All-beautiful; sole Reality and ultimate controlling Power of the whole? This is not a figure of speech; this is a fact. The fact of Gravitation known to all animals, is not surer than this inner Fact, which may be known to all men. He who knows this, it will sink, silent, awful, unspeakable, into his heart. He will say with Faust: "Who *dare* name Him?" Most rituals or 'namings' he will fall in with at present, are like to be 'namings'—which shall be nameless! In silence, in the Eternal Temple, let him worship, if there be no fit word. Such knowledge, the crown of his whole spiritual being, the life of his life, let him keep and sacredly walk by. He has a religion. Hourly and daily, for himself and for the whole world, a faithful, unspoken, but not ineffectual prayer rises, "Thy will be done." His whole work on Earth is an emblematic spoken or acted prayer, Be the will of God done on Earth,—not the Devil's will, or any of the Devil's servants' wills! He has a religion, this man; an everlasting Loadstar that beams the brighter in the Heavens, the darker here on Earth grows the night around him. Thou, if thou know not this, what are all rituals, liturgies, mythologies, mass-chantings, turnings of the rotatory calabash? They are as nothing; in a good many respects they are as *less*. Divorced from this, getting half-divorced from this, they are a thing to fill one with a kind of horror; with a sacred inexpressible pity and fear. The most tragical thing a human eye can look on. It was said to the Prophet, "Behold, I will shew thee worse things than these: women weeping to Thammuz." That was the acme of the Prophet's vision—then as now.

Rituals, Liturgies, Credos, Sinai Thunder: I know more or less the history of these; the rise, progress, decline and fall of these. Can thunder from all the thirty-two azimuths, repeated daily for centuries of years, make God's Laws more godlike to me? Brother, No. Perhaps I am grown to be a man now; and do not need the thunder and the terror any longer! Perhaps I am above being frightened; perhaps it is not Fear, but Reverence alone, that shall now lead me!—Revelations, Inspirations? Yes: and thy own god-created Soul; dost thou not call that a 'revelation?' Who made THEE? Where didst Thou come from? The Voice of Eternity, if thou be not a blasphemer and poor asphyxied mute, speaks with that tongue of thine! *Thou* art the latest Birth of Nature; it is 'the Inspiration of the Almighty' that giveth *thee* understanding! My brother, my brother!—

Under baleful Atheisms, Mammonisms, Joe-Manton Dilettantisms, with their appropriate Cants and Idolisms, and whatsoever scandalous rubbish obscures and all but extinguishes the soul of man,—religion now is; its Laws, written if not on stone tables, yet on the Azure of Infinitude, in the inner heart of God's Creation, certain as Life, certain as Death! I say the Laws are there, and thou shalt not disobey them. It were better for thee not. Better a hundred deaths than yes. Terrible 'penalties' withal, if thou still need 'penalties' are there for disobeying. Dost thou observe, O redtape Politician, that fiery infernal Phenomenon, which men name FRENCH REVOLUTION, sailing unlooked-for, unbidden; through thy inane Protocol Dominion:—far-seen, with splendour not of Heaven? Ten centuries will see it. There were Tanneries at Meudon for human skins. And Hell, very truly Hell, had power over God's upper Earth for a season. The crudest Portent that has risen into created Space these ten centuries: let us hail it, with awestruck repentant hearts, as the voice once more of a God, though of one in wrath. Blessed be the God's voice;

The Modern Worker

for it *is* true, and Falsehoods have to cease before it! But for that same preternatural quasi-infernal Portent, one could not know what to make of this wretched world, in these days, at all. The deplorablest quack-ridden, and now hunger-ridden, downtrodden Despicability and *Flebile Ludibrium* ["sad mockery"], of red-tape Protocols, rotatory Calabashes, Poor-Law Bastilles: who is there that could think of *its* being fated to continue?—

Penalties enough, my brother! This penalty inclusive of all: Eternal Death to thy own hapless Self, if thou heed no other. Eternal Death, I say,—with many meanings old and new, of which let this single one suffice us here: The eternal impossibility for thee to be aught but a Chimera, and swift-vanishing deceptive Phantasm, in God's Creation;—swift-vanishing, never to reappear: why should *it* reappear! Thou hadst one chance, thou wilt never have another. Everlasting-ages will roll on, and no other be given thee. The foolishest articulate-speaking soul now extant, may not he say to himself: "A whole Eternity I waited to be born; and now I have a whole Eternity waiting to see what I will do when born!" This is not Theology, this is Arithmetic. And thou but half-discernest this; thou but half believest it? Alas, on the shores of the Dead Sea on Sabbath there goes on a Tragedy!—

But we will leave this of 'Religion;' of which, to say truth, it is chiefly profitable in these unspeakable days to keep silence. Thou needest no 'New Religion;' nor art thou like to get any. Thou hast already more 'religion' than thou makest use of. This day, thou knowest ten commanded duties, seest in thy mind ten things which should be done, for one that thou doest! *Do* one of them; this of itself will shew thee ten others which can and shall be done. "But my future fate?" Yes, thy future fate, indeed? Thy future fate, while thou makest *it* the chief question, seems to me—extremely questionable! I do not think it can be good. Norse Odin, immemorial centuries ago, did not he, though a poor Heathen, in the dawn of Time, teach us that for the Dastard there was, and could be, no good fate; no harbour anywhere, save down with Hela, in the pool of Night! Dastards, Knaves, are they that lust for Pleasure, that tremble at Pain. For this world and for the next, Dastards are a class of creatures made to be 'arrested:' they are good for nothing else, can look for nothing else. A greater than Odin has been here. A greater than Odin has taught us—not a greater Dastardism, I hope! My brother, thou must pray for a *soul*; struggle, as with life-and-death energy, to get back thy soul! Know that 'religion' is no Morrison's Pill from without, but a reawakening of thy own Self from within:—and, above all, leave me alone of thy 'religions' and 'new religions' here and elsewhere! I am weary of this sick croaking for a Morrison's-Pill religion; for any and for every such. I want none such; and discern all such to be impossible. The resuscitation of old liturgies fallen dead; much more, the manufacture of new liturgies that will never be alive: how hopeless! Stylitisms, eremite fanaticisms and fakeerisms; spasmodic agonistic posture-makings, and narrow, cramped, morbid, if forever noble wrestlings: all this is not a thing desirable to me. It is a thing the world *has* done once,—when its beard was not grown as now!

And yet there is, at worst, one Liturgy which does remain forever unexceptionable: that of *Praying* (as the old Monks did withal) *by Working*. And indeed the Prayer which accomplished itself in special chapels at stated hours, and went not with a man, rising up from all his Work and Action, at all moments sanctifying the same,—what was it ever good for? 'Work is Worship:' yes, in a highly considerable sense,—which, in the present state of all 'worship,' who is there that can unfold! He that understands it well, understands the Prophecy of the whole Future; the last Evangel, which has included all others. *Its* cathedral the Dome of Immensity,—hast thou seen it? coped with the star-galaxies; paved with the green mosaic of land and ocean; and for altar, verily, the Star-throne of the Eternal! Its litany and psalmody the noble acts, the heroic work and suffering, and true heart-utterance of all the Valiant of the Sons of Men. Its choir-music the ancient Winds and Oceans, and deep-toned, inarticulate, but most speaking voices of Destiny and History,—supernal ever as of old. Between two great Silences:

> 'Stars silent rest o'er us,
> Graves under us silent.'

Between which two great Silences, do not, as we said, all human Noises, in the naturalest times, most *preter*naturally march and roll?—

I will insert this also, in a lower strain, from Sauerteig's *Es-*

thetische Springwürzel ["Aesthetic Start-roots"]. 'Worship?' says he: 'Before that inane tumult of Hearsay filled men's heads, while the world lay yet silent, and the heart true and open, many things were Worship! To the primeval man whatsoever good came, descended on him (as, in mere fact, it ever does) direct from God; whatsoever duty lay visible for him, this a Supreme God had prescribed. To the present hour I ask thee, Who else? For the primeval man, in whom dwelt Thought, this Universe was all a Temple; Life everywhere a Worship.

'What Worship, for example, is there not in mere Washing! Perhaps one of the most moral things a man, in common cases, has it in his power to do. Strip thyself, go into the bath, or were it into the limpid pool and running brook, and there wash and be clean; thou wilt step out again a purer and a better man. This consciousness of perfect outer pureness, that to thy skin there now adheres no foreign Deck of imperfection, how it radiates in on thee, with cunning symbolic influences, to thy very soul! Thou hast an increase of tendency towards all good things whatsoever. The oldest Eastern Sages, with joy and holy gratitude, had felt it so,—and that it was the Maker's gift and will. Whose else is it? It remains a religious duty, from oldest times, in the East.—Nor could Herr Professor Strauss, when I put the question, deny that for us at present it is still such here in the West! To that dingy fuliginous Operative, emerging from his soot-mill, what is the first duty I will prescribe, and offer help towards? That he clean the skin of him. *Can* he pray, by any ascertained method? One knows not entirely:—but with soap and a sufficiency of water, he can wash. Even the dull English feel something of this; they have a saying, "Cleanliness is near of kin to Godliness:"—yet never, in any country, saw I operative men worse washed, and, in a climate drenched with the softest cloud-water, such a scarcity of baths!'—

Alas, Sauerteig, our 'operative men' are at present short even of potatoes: what 'duty' can you prescribe to them!

Or let us give a glance at China. Our new friend, the Emperor there, is Pontiff of three hundred million men; who do all live and work, these many centuries now; authentically patronised by Heaven so far; and therefore must have some 'religion' of a kind. This Emperor-Pontiff has, in fact, a religious belief of certain Laws of Heaven; observes, with a religious rigour, his 'three thousand punctualities' given out by men of insight, some sixty generations since, as a legible transcript of the same,—the Heavens do seem to say, not totally an incorrect one. He has not much of a ritual, this Pontiff-Emperor; believes, it is likest? with the old Monks, that 'Labour is Worship.' His most public Act of Worship, it appears, is the drawing solemnly at a certain day, on the green bosom of our Mother Earth, when the Heavens, after dead black winter, have again with their vernal radiances awakened her, a distinct red Furrow with the Plough,—signal that all the Ploughs of China are to begin ploughing and worshipping! It is notable enough. He, in sight of the Seen and Unseen Powers, draws his distinct red Furrow there; saying, and praying, in mute symbolism, so many most eloquent things!

If you ask this Pontiff, "Who made him? What is to become of him and us?" he maintains a dignified reserve; waves his hand and pontiff-eyes over the unfathomable deep of Heaven, the 'Tsien,' the azure kingdoms of Infinitude; as if asking, "Is it doubtful that we are right well made? Can aught that is *wrong* become of us?"—He and his three hundred millions (it is their chief 'punctuality') visit yearly the Tombs of their Fathers; each man the Tomb of his Father and his Mother; alone there, in silence, with what of 'worship' or of other thought there may be, pauses solemnly each man; the divine Skies all silent over him; the divine Graves, and this divinest Grave, all silent under him; the pulsing of his own soul, if he have any soul, alone audible. Truly it may be a kind of worship! Truly, if a man cannot get some glimpse into the Eternities, looking through this portal,—through what other need he try it?

Our friend the Pontiff-Emperor permits cheerfully, though with contempt, all manner of Buddists, Bonzes, Talapoins and such like, to build brick Temples, on the voluntary principle; to worship with what of chantings, paper-lanterns and tumultuous brayings, pleases them; and make night hideous, since they find some comfort in so doing. Cheerfully, though with contempt. He is a wiser Pontiff than many persons think! He is as yet the one Chief Potentate or Priest in this Earth who has made a distinct systematic attempt at what we call the ultimate result of all religion, '*Practical* Hero-worship:' he does incessantly, with true anxiety, in such way as he can, search and sift (it would appear) his whole enormous population for the Wisest born among them; by which Wisest, as by born Kings, these three hundred million men are governed. The Heavens, to a certain extent, do appear to countenance him. These three hundred millions actually make porcelain, souchong tea, with innumerable other things; and fight, under Heaven's flag, against Necessity;— and have fewer Seven-Years Wars, Thirty-Years Wars, French Revolution Wars, and infernal fightings with each other, than certain millions elsewhere have!

Nay, in our poor distracted Europe itself, in these newest times, have there not religious voices risen,—with a religion new and yet the oldest; entirely indisputable to all hearts of men? Some I do know, who did not call or think themselves 'Prophets,' far enough from that; but who were, in very truth, melodious Voices from the eternal Heart of Nature once again; souls forever venerable to all that have a soul, A French Revolution is one phenomenon; as complement and spiritual exponent thereof, a Poet Goethe and German Literature is to me another. The old Secular or Practical World, so to speak, having gone up in fire, is not here the prophecy and dawn of a new Spiritual World, parent of far nobler, wider, new Practical Worlds? A life of Antique devoutness, Antique veracity and heroism, has again become possible, is again seen actual there, for the most modern man. A phenomenon, as quiet as it is, comparable for greatness to no other! 'The great event 'for the world is, now as always, the arrival in it of a new 'Wise Man.' Touches there are, be the Heavens ever thanked, of new Sphere-melody; audible once more, in the infinite jargoning discords and poor scrannel-pipings of the thing called Literature:—priceless there, as the voice of new Heavenly Psalms! Literature, like the old Prayer-Collections of the first centuries, were it 'well selected from and burnt,' contains precious things. For Literature, with all its printing-presses, puffing-engines and shoreless deafening triviality, *is* yet 'the Thought of Thinking Souls.' A sacred 'religion,' if you like the name, does live in the heart of that strange froth-ocean, not wholly froth, which we call Literature; and will more and more disclose itself therefrom;—not now as scorching Fire: the red smoky scorching Fire has purified itself into white sunny Light. Is not Light grander than Fire? It is the same element in a state of purity.

My ingenuous readers, we will march out of this Third Book

with a rhythmic word of Goethe's on our lips; a word which perhaps has already sung itself, in dark hours and in bright, through many a heart. To me, finding it devout yet wholly credible and veritable, full of piety yet free of cant; to me joyfully finding much in it, and joyfully missing so much in it, this little snatch of music, by the greatest German Man, sounds like a stanza in the grand *Road-Song* and *Marching-Song* of our great Teutonic Kindred, wending, wending, valiant and victorious, through the undiscovered Deeps of Time! He calls it *Mason-Lodge*,—not Psalm or Hymn:

> The Mason's ways are
> A type of Existence,
> And his persistence
> Is as the days are
> Of men in this world.
>
> The Future hides in it
> Gladness and sorrow;
> We press still thorow,
> Nought that abides in it
> Daunting us,—onward.
>
> And solemn before us,
> Veiled, the dark Portal,
> Goal of all mortal:—
> Stars silent rest o'er us,
> Graves under us silent.
>
> While earnest thou gazest,
> Comes boding of terror,
> Comes phantasm and error,
> Perplexes the bravest
> With doubt and misgiving.
>
> But heard are the Voices,—
> Heard are the Sages,
> The Worlds and the Ages:
> "Choose well, your choice is
> Brief and yet endless:
>
> Here eyes do regard you,
> In Eternity's stillness;

The Modern Worker

Here is all fulness,
Ye brave, to reward you:
Work, and despair not?"

Glossary

All entries taken from *The Nuttall Encyclopaedia* 1907 ed., except where indicated. † indicates an entry original to this edition.

Anarchy plus a street constable:† Carlyle's description of classical liberalism.

Apes, Dead Sea: Dwellers by the Dead Sea who, according to the Moslem tradition, were transformed into apes because they turned a deaf ear to God's message to them by the lips of Moses, fit symbol, thinks Carlyle, of many in modern time to whom the universe, with all its serious voices, seems to have become a weariness and a humbug.

Articles, the Thirty-Nine: Originally Forty-Two, a creed framed in 1562, which every clergyman of the Church of England is bound by law to subscribe to at his ordination, as the accepted faith of the Church.

Asphyxia: Suspended respiration in the physical life; a term frequently employed by Carlyle to denote a much more recondite, but a no less real, corresponding phenomenon in the spiritual life.

Black Dobbin:† Carlyle uses the relationship between farmer and horse to illustrate that between master and labourer throughout his work, particularly in *Latter-Day Pamphlets*. In *Occasional Discourse* Carlyle personifies this relationship as between Farmer Hodge and his horse, Black Dobbin.

Bradshaw, John: President of the High Court of Justice for trial of Charles I, born at Stockport; bred for the bar; a friend of Milton; a thorough republican, and opposed to the Protectorate; became president of the Council on

Cromwell's death; was buried in Westminster; his body was exhumed and hung in chains at the Restoration (1586-1659).

Bridgewater Bequest:[1] The late Earl of Bridgewater left £8,000 for the production of a work having for its object the exemplification of the "Wisdom of God in the Creation;" a noble sum, and a noble object.

Bonze: A Buddhist priest in China, Japan, Burmah, &c.

Brindley, James: A mechanician and engineer, born in Derbyshire; bred a millwright; devoted his skill and genius to the construction of canals, under the patronage of the Duke of Bridgewater, as the greatest service he could render to his country; regarded rivers as mere "feeders to canals" (1716-1772).

Bull, John: A humorous impersonation of the collective English people, conceived of as well-fed, good-natured, honest-hearted, justice-loving, and plain-spoken; the designation is derived from Arbuthnot's satire, *The History of John Bull*, in which the Church of England figures as his mother.

Cagliostro, Count Alessandro di: Assumed name of an arch-impostor, his real name being Giuseppe Balsamo, born in Palermo, of poor parents; early acquired a smattering of chemistry and medicine, by means of which he perpetrated the most audacious frauds, which, when detected in one place were repeated with even more brazen effrontery in another; married a pretty woman named Lorenza Feliciani, who became an accomplice; professed supernatural powers, and wrung large sums from his dupes wherever they went, after which they absconded to Paris and lived in extravagance; here he was thrown into the Bastille for complicity in the diamond necklace affair; on his wife turning informer, he was consigned to the tender mercies of the Inquisition, and committed to the fortress of San Leone, where he died at 52, his wife having retired into a convent (1743-1795).

Calabash of the Calmucks:[2] Their prayer-barrel, Kūrūdu, is

---

1 From *The Spectator*, 1832.
2 From Tait, William, *Carlyle's German Romance: Specimens of its*

Glossary

a hollowed shell, a calabash, full of unrolled formulas of prayer; they sway it from side to side, and then it works. More philosophically viewed, since in prayer the feeling only is of consequence, it is much the same whether this express itself by motion of the mouth or of the calabash.

Caliban: A slave in Shakespeare's *Tempest*, of the grossest animality of nature.

Cameronians: A Presbyterian body in Scotland who derived their name from Richard Cameron, contended like him for the faith to which the nation by covenant had bound itself, and even declined to take the oath of allegiance to sovereigns such as William III and his successors, who did not explicitly concede to the nation this right.

Carlton Club: The Conservative club in London, so called, as erected on the site of Carlton House, demolished in 1828, and occupied by George IV when he was Prince of Wales.

Cavaignac, Louis Eugene: A distinguished French general, born in Paris; appointed governor of Algeria in 1849, but recalled to be head of the executive power in Paris same year; appointed dictator, suppressed the insurrection in June, after the most obstinate and bloody struggle the streets of Paris had witnessed since the first Revolution; stood candidate for the Presidency, to which Louis Napoleon was elected; was arrested after the *coup d'etat*, but soon released; never gave in his adherence to the Empire (1802-1857).

Chandos-Clause:[3] The enfranchisement of the £50 tenant-at-will in the counties (cl. XX). This was the so-called Chandos clause (from the name of its mover, Lord Chandos) which received support not only from country gentry anxious to strengthen landlord and agricultural interests but also from radicals favouring any extension of the suffrage.

Chartism: A movement of the working-classes of Great Britain for greater political power than was conceded to them by the Reform Bill of 1832, and which found

Chief Authors (1841).
3 From Norman Gash, *The Age of Peel* (1973).

expression in a document called the "People's Charter," drawn up in 1838, embracing six "points," as they were called, viz., Manhood Suffrage, Equal Electoral Districts, Vote by Ballot, Annual Parliaments, Abolition of a Property Qualification in the Parliamentary Representation, and Payment of Members of Parliament, all which took the form of a petition presented to the House of Commons in 1839, and signed by 1,380,000 persons. The refusal of the petition gave rise to great agitation over the country, which gradually died out in 1848.

Cherusci: An ancient people of Germany, whose leader was Arminius, and under whom they defeated the Romans, commanded by Varus, in 9 A.D.

Chocktaws, or Chactaws: A tribe of American Indians, settled to civilised life in the Indian Territory, U.S.; the Chactaw Indian, with his proud array of scalps hung up in his wigwam, is, with Carlyle, the symbol of the pride of wealth acquired at the price of the lives of men in body and soul.

Cleon: An Athenian demagogue, surnamed the Tanner, from his profession, which he forsook that he might champion the rights of the people; rose in popular esteem by his victory over the Spartans, but being sent against Brasidas, the Spartan general, was defeated and fell in the battle, 422 B.C.; is regarded by Thucydides with disfavour, and by Aristophanes with contempt, but both these writers were of the aristocracy, and possibly prejudiced, though the object of their disfavour had many of the marks of the vulgar agitator, and stands for the type of one.

Clothes: Carlyle's name in *Sartor Resartus* for the guises which the spirit, especially of man, weaves for itself and wears, and by which it both conceals itself in shame and reveals itself in grace.

Constable: A high officer of State in the Roman empire, in France, and in England, charged at one time with military, judicial, and regulative functions.

Corn-Laws: Laws in force in Great Britain regulating the import and export of corn for the protection of the home-producer at the expense of the home-consumer, and which after a long and bitter struggle between these two classes were abolished in 1846.

Court of Requests:[4] In England, one of the prerogative courts that grew out of the king's council (Curia Regis) in the late 15th century. The court's primary function was to deal with civil petitions from poor people and the king's servants.

Covenant, The National: A solemn engagement on the part of the Scottish nation subscribed to by all ranks of the community, the first signature being appended to it in the Greyfriars' Churchyard, Edinburgh, on February 28, 1638, to maintain the Presbyterian Church and to resist all attempts on the part of Charles I to foist Episcopacy upon it; it was ratified by the Scottish Parliament in 1640, and subscribed by Charles II in 1650 and 1651.

Covenanters: A body of strict Presbyterians who held out against the breach of the Solemn League and Covenant (see above).

Crabbe, George: An English poet, born at Aldborough, in Suffolk […] his principal poems are *The Library*, *The Village*, *The Parish Register*, *The Borough*, and the *Tales of the Hall*, all, particularly the earlier ones, instinct with interest in the lives of the poor, "the sacrifices, temptations, loves, and crimes of humble life," described with the most "unrelenting" realism; the author in Byron's esteem, "though Nature's sternest painter, yet the best".

Dahomey: A negro kingdom of undefined limits, and under French protectorate, in W. Africa, N. of the Slave Coast; the religious rites of the natives are sanguinary, they offer human victims in sacrifice; is an agricultural country, yields palm-oil and gold dust, and once a great centre of the slave-trade.

Davies, Howel:[5] Howell Davis (ca. 1690 – 19 June 1719), also known as Hywel and/or Davies, was a Welsh pirate. His piratical career lasted just 11 months, from 11 July 1718 to 19 June 1719, when he was ambushed and killed.

Delf-Platter:[†] Delftware, AKA faience, a type of decorative

---

4 From *Britannica*, retrieved 2021.
5 From *Wikipedia*, retrieved 2021.

tin-glazed pottery.

Delolme, John Louis: A writer on State polity, born at Geneva, bred to the legal profession; spent some six years in England as a refugee; wrote a book on *The Constitution of England*, and in praise of it, which was received for a time with high favour in the country, but is now no longer regarded as an authority; wrote a *History of the Flagellants*, and on *The Union of Scotland with England* (1740-1806).

Dilettantism: An idle, often affected, almost always barren admiration and study of the fine arts, "in earnest about nothing."

Dismal Science: Carlyle's name for the political economy that with self-complacency leaves everything to settle itself by the law of supply and demand, as if that were all the law and the prophets. The name is applied to every science that affects to dispense with the spiritual as a ruling factor in human affairs.

Dogger Bank: A sandbank in the North Sea; a great fishing-field, extending between Jutland in Denmark and Yorkshire in England, though distant from both shores, 170 m. long, over 60 m. broad, and from 8 to 10 fathoms deep.

Drury Lane: A celebrated London theatre founded in 1663, in what was a fashionable quarter of the city then; has since that time been thrice burnt down; was the scene of Garrick's triumphs, and of those of many of his illustrious successors, though it is now given up chiefly to pantomimes and spectacular exhibitions.

Dryasdust: A name of Sir Walter Scott's invention, and employed by him to denote an imaginary character who supplied him with dry preliminary historical details, and since used to denote a writer who treats a historical subject with all due diligence and research, but without any appreciation of the human interest in it, still less the soul of it.

Eastcheap:[6] Eastcheap is a street in central London that is a western continuation of Great Tower Street towards Monument junction. Its name derives from cheap, the

---

[6] From *Wikipedia*, retrieved 2021.

Old English word for market, with the prefix 'East' distinguishing it from Westcheap, another former market street that today is called Cheapside.

Edmund, St.: King or "landlord" of East Anglia from 855 to 870; refused to renounce Christianity and accept heathenism at the hands of a set of "mere physical force" invading Danes, and suffered martyrdom rather; was made a saint of and had a monastery called "Bury St. Edmunds," in Norfolk, raised to his memory over his grave.

Emancipation: Originally a term in Roman law and name given to the process of the manumission of a son by his father; the son was sold to a third party and after the sale became *sui juris*; it is now applied to the remission of old laws in the interest of freedom, which Carlyle regards in his *Shooting Niagara*, as the sum of nearly all modern recent attempts at Reform.

Eternities, The Conflux of: Carlyle's expressive phrase for Time, as in every moment of it a centre in which all the forces to and from Eternity meet and unite, so that by no past and no future can we be brought nearer to Eternity than where we at any moment of Time are; the Present Time, the youngest born of Eternity, being the child and heir of all the Past times with their good and evil, and the parent of all the Future, the import of which (see Matt. xvi. 27) it is accordingly the first and most sacred duty of every successive age, and especially the leaders of it, to know and lay to heart as the only link by which Eternity lays hold of it and it of Eternity.

Gehenna: The valley of Hinnom, on the S. of Jerusalem, with Tophet at its eastern end; became the symbol of hell from the fires kept burning in it night and day to consume the poisonous gases of the offal accumulated in it.

Golconda: A fortified town in the Nizam's dominions, 7 m. W. of Hyderabad; famous for its diamonds, found in the neighbourhood; beside it are the ruins of the ancient city, the former capital of the old kingdom; the fort is garrisoned, and is the treasury of the Nizam; it is also a State prison.

Guthlac, St.:[7] One of the most famous saints from the early period of Christianity in Britain. [...] Guthlac lived a life of penance: he fasted every day, only eating barley bread and drinking marshy water in the evenings, and wore simple animal skins for clothing. He was often tormented by demons and the descriptions of these devils in the earliest account of his life are vivid and terrifying.

Gwynn, Nell: A "pretty, witty" actress of Drury Lane, who became mistress of Charles II, whose son by her was created Duke of St. Albans; the king was very fond of her and took special thought of her when he was dying (1640–1691).

Hampden, John: A famous English statesman and patriot, cousin to Oliver Cromwell, born in London; passed through Oxford and studied law at the Inner Temple; subsequently he settled down on his father's estate, and in 1621 entered Parliament, joining the opposition; he came first into conflict with the king by refusing to contribute to a general loan levied by Charles, and subsequently became famous by his resistance to the ship-money tax; he was a member of the Short Parliament, and played a prominent part in the more eventful transactions of the Long Parliament; an attempt on Charles's part to seize Hampden and four other members precipitated the Civil War; he took an active part in organising the Parliamentary forces, and proved himself a brave and skilful general in the field; he fell mortally wounded while opposing Prince Rupert in a skirmish at Chalgrove Field; historians unite in extolling his nobility of character, statesmanship, and single-minded patriotism (1594–1643).

Hansard: Record of the proceedings and debates in the British Parliament, published by the printers Hansard, the founder of the firm being Luke Hansard, a printer of Norwich, who came to London in 1770 as a compositor, and succeeded as proprietor of the business in which he was a workman; *d.* 1828.

Healing Parliament:[†] Harbottle Grimston's description of the Convention Parliament of 1660.

---

7 From the British Library, retrieved 2021.

Glossary

Heathenism: As defined by Carlyle, "plurality of gods, mere sensuous representation of the Mystery of Life, and for chief recognised element therein Physical Force, as contrasted with Christianism, or Faith in an Invisible, not as real only, but as the only reality; Time, through every meanest moment of it, resting on Eternity; Pagan empire of Force displaced by a nobler supremacy, that of Holiness."

Heavyside:† Carlyle's name for the solid and commonsensical Englishman.

Heavy-Wet:[8] Malt liquor, because the more a man drinks of it, the heavier and more stupid he becomes.

Heptarchy, Anglo-Saxon: The seven kingdoms of Kent, Sussex, Wessex, Essex, Northumberland, East Anglia, and Mercia, the chief of those established by the Saxons during the 6th century in Great Britain.

High Life Below Stairs:† A 1759 comedy play by the British writer James Townley.

Histrionism:[9] Carlyle distinguishes between histrionism and heroism by reference to Napoleon Bonaparte and Oliver Cromwell respectively [...] † Carlyle saw Napoleon as histrionic and theatrical.

Hodge: See Black Dobbin.

Horologe: Archaism for clock or watch.

Howel-and-Jameses:[10] Howell James & Company was a firm of jewellers and silversmiths based in Regent Street in London which operated between 1819 and 1911.

Hel or **Hela:** In Scandinavian mythology an inexorable divinity, the death-goddess who presides over the icy realm of the dead; her maw was insatiable and her heart pitiless.

Herschel, Sir William: A distinguished astronomer, born at Hanover; son of a musician, and bred to the profession;

---

8 From John Camden Hotten, *A Dictionary of Modern Slang, Cant, and Vulgar Words* (1867).
9 From Harnick, Phyllis, *Carlyle and Mill on Ireland in 1848*, Caryle Newsletter (1986).
10 From *Wikipedia*, retrieved 2021.

came to England at the end of the Seven Years' War, and obtained sundry appointments as an organist; gave his leisure time to the study of astronomy and survey of the heavens; discovered the planet Uranus in 1781, which he called *Georgium sidus* in honour of George III, discovered also the two innermost belts of Saturn, as well as drew up a catalogue of 5000 heavenly bodies or clusters of them (1738-1822).

Idolatry: Worship paid to a mere symbol of the divine while the heart is dead to all sense of that which it symbolises; a species of offence against the Most High, of which many are flagrantly guilty who affect to regard with pity the worshipper of idols of wood or stone. "Idolatry," says Buskin, *apropos* of Carlyle's well-known doctrine, "is summed up in the one broad wickedness of refusing to worship Force and resolving to worship No-Force; denying the Almighty, and bowing down to four-and-twopence with a stamp on it."

Io Pæan:[11] A hymn to Apollo, and applied to the god himself. We are told in Dr. Smith's *Classical Dictionary*, that this word is from *Paean*, the physician of the Olympian gods; but surely it could be no honour to the Sun-god to be called by the name of his own vassal. Hermsterhuis suggests *pauo*, to make to cease, meaning to make diseases to cease; but why supply diseases rather than any other noun? The more likely derivation, *me judice*, is the Greek verb *paio*, to dart; Apollo being called the "far-darter." The hymn began with "*Io Paean*." Homer applies it to a triumphal song in general.

Kauderwälsch von Pferdefuss-quacksalber, Herr Ritter:[†] ["Mr. Knight Gibberish of Horsefoot-Mountebank"], probably a reference to Robert Peel (English statesman and founder of the Metropolitan Police service).[12] The opposition to the revised sliding scale was personified by the Duke of Buckingham and Chandos, who had resigned as Lord-Keeper of the Privy Seal early in the session in protest against Peel's ("his Excellenz the Titular-Herr Ritter Kauderwälsch von Pferdefuss-Quacksal-

---

11 From E. Cobham Brewer, *Dictionary of Phrase and Fable* (1894).
12 From Altick, Richard D., *Carlyle and His Contemporaries* (1976).

Glossary

ber'"s, p. 215) wooing of the Manchester bloc.

Kentish Fire: Vehement and prolonged derisive cheering, so called from indulgence in it in Kent at meetings to oppose the Catholic Emancipation Bill of 1829.

Kircher, Athanasius:† A Jesuit polymath who developed an early version of the projector and treated of optics in his *Ars Magna Lucis et Umbrae*.

Lamartine, Alphonse Marie de: A French author, politician, and poet, born in Macon; his poetic effusions procured for him admission into the French Academy, and in 1834 he entered the Chamber of Deputies [...] after serving in the Provisional Government of 1848 he stood candidate for the Presidency, but was defeated, and on the occasion of the coup d'etat, he retired into private life.

Literature: Defined by Carlyle "as an 'apocalypse of nature,' a revealing of the 'open secret,' a 'continuous revelation' of the God-like in the terrestrial and common, which ever endures there, and is brought out now in this dialect, now in that, with various degrees of clearness!... there being touches of it (i.e. the God-like) in the dark stormful indignation of a Byron, nay, in the withered mockery of a French sceptic, his mockery of the false, a love and worship of the true ... how much more in the sphere harmony of a Shakespeare, the cathedral music of a Milton; something of it too in those humble, genuine, lark-notes of a Burns, skylark starting from the humble furrow far overhead into the blue depths, and singing to us so genuinely there."

Louis-Philippe Joseph: [A duke of Orleans], surnamed Philippe-Egalite, played a conspicuous part in the Revolution, and perished on the scaffold (1747-1793).

Manton, Joe:† A British gunsmith, bankrupted by a series of legal battles over non-payment by the British military for a sale.

Mark, England Her:† Most likely a reference to the supposed Germanic system of land tenure.[13] The name given to a social organization which rests on the common ten-

---

13 From *Britannica* (1911).

ure and common cultivation of the land by small groups of freemen. Both politically and economically the mark was an independent community, and its earliest members were doubtless blood relatives. In its origin the word is the same as mark or march, a boundary.

M'Croudy The Seraphic Doctor:[†] J. R. McCulloch, Scottish economist and intellectual successor to David Ricardo, a pioneer in the field of econometrics.

Megatherion:[14] An extinct genus of ground sloths endemic to South America that lived from the Early Pliocene through the end of the Pleistocene.

Melton-Mowbray: A town 15 m. NE. of Leicester, the centre of the great hunting district; celebrated for its pork pies.

Mene, Mene:[†] A shorthand for Mene, Mene, Tekel, Peres ["number, number, weight, division"], the writing on the wall in *Daniel* 5:26–28, interpreted to mean "God hath numbered thy kingdom, and finished it. Thou art weighed in the balances, and art found wanting. Thy kingdom is divided, and given to the Medes and Persians."

Meudon, Tanneries of:[15] What people in Europe does not take as a fable the establishment of the tannery of human skin at Meudon? Nonetheless one remembers that a man came to the bar of the Convention to announce a new and simple procedure for procuring an abondance of leather; that the Committee of Public Safety granted him the locale of the Chateau de Meudon, whose doors were carefully closed, and that finally several members of this committee were the first to wear boots made of human leather.

Mights and Rights: The Carlyle doctrine that Rights are nothing till they have realised and established themselves as Mights; they are rights first only then.

Morrison's Pills: A form of quackery. From the British College of Health: it began in 1825 as a campaign conducted

---

14 From *Wikipedia*, retrieved 2021.
15 From Dusaulchoy de Bergemont, *Mosaique Histoirque, Litteraire et Politique* (1818).

Glossary

by James Morison to assert the importance of the blood; he believed that all diseases were caused by its impurity, and therefore urged the necessity of purging it with vegetables, with his own specially-developed Vegetable Pill.

Necker, Jacques: Celebrated financier, born at Geneva, banker in Paris; married the accomplished Susanne Curchod, the rejected of Gibbon, and became by her the father of Mme. de Stael; was a man of high repute for probity and business capacity; became in 1777 Director-General of Finance in France, tried hard and honestly, by borrowing and retrenchment, to restore the fallen public credit, but was after five years dismissed; was recalled in 1788, but though the funds rose, and he contributed to their relief two million livres of his own money, was again dismissed, to be once more recalled, only to expose his inability to cope with the crisis and to be forced to retire (1732–1804).

Operatives:† Dated term for a worker; "Manchester operatives" formed a union in the 1830s, eventually securing a half-day off on Saturday.

Orcus: [i.e. place of confinement], another name for Hades, or the "World of the Dead"; also of the god of the nether world.

Ou' Clo':[16] From the early 1830s, Carlyle used variants of the phrase "Hebrew old-clothes" as metaphorical reference to the fabric of Judeo-Christian beliefs that had once clothed authentic spiritual truths but were now, in his view, worn-out tatters that needed replacing if there were to be true spiritual rebirth in Britain and the modern world more generally. As late as 1850, Carlyle still hoped for such a transformation, writing in "Jesuitism," the last of the *Latter-Day Pamphlets*, "we shall all yet make our Exodus from Houndsditch [the district in the east end of London noted for its used-clothing shops and Jewish clothes merchants], and bid the sordid continents, of once rich apparel now grown poisonous Ou'-clo' [old clothes], a mild farewell."

Owen's Labour-Bank:† Carlyle's name for the labour ex-

---

16 From Kerry et al., *Thomas Carlyle and the Idea of Influence* (2018).

changes established by Robert Owen in the 1830s, having as their principal object the effective distribution of labour.

Park, Mungo: African traveller, born at Foulshiels, near Selkirk; was apprenticed to a surgeon, and studied medicine at Edinburgh; 1791–93 he spent in a voyage to Sumatra, and in 1795 went for the first time to Africa under the auspices of the African Association of London; starting from the Gambia he penetrated eastward to the Niger, then westward to Kamalia, where illness seized him; conveyed to his starting-point by a slave-trader, he returned to England and published *Travels in the Interior of Africa*, 1799; he married and settled to practice at Peebles, but he was not happy till in 1805 he set out for Africa again at Government expense; starting from Pisania he reached the Niger, and sending back his journals attempted to descend the river in a canoe, but, attacked by natives, the canoe overturned; and he and his companions were drowned (1771–1805).

Parcae: The Roman name of the three fates, derived from "pars," a part, as apportioning to every individual his destiny.

Patent-Digester:[†] A forerunner to the pressure cooker, invented in 1679 by Denis Papin. Carlyle uses the image as a metaphor for man as mere stomach, or machine.

Piepowder Court:[17] A court of piepowders was a special tribunal in England organized by a borough on the occasion of a fair or market. These courts had unlimited jurisdiction over personal actions for events taking place in the market, including disputes between merchants, theft, and acts of violence.

Pitt, William, Earl of Chatham: A great British statesman and orator, born in Cornwall; determined opponent of Sir Robert Walpole; succeeded in driving him from power, and at length installing himself in his place; had an eye to the greatness and glory of England, summoned the English nation to look to its laurels; saw the French, the rivals of England, beaten back in the four quarters of the

---

17 From *Wikipedia*, retrieved 2021.

globe […] "for four years" (of his life), says Carlyle, "king of England; never again he; never again one resembling him, nor indeed can ever be."

Pleas of the Crown, Four:[18] The (four) pleas of the Crown, Legal proceedings on matters over which the Crown claimed an exclusive criminal jurisdiction, in Scot. applied only to murder, robbery, rape and fire-raising.

Plugston of Undershot: Carlyle's name in *Past and Present* for a member or "Master-Worker" of the English mammon-worshipping manufacturing class in rivalry with the aristocracy for the ascendency in the land, who pays his workers his wages and thinks he has done his duty with them in so doing, and is secure in the fortune he has made by that cash-payment gospel of his as all the law and the prophets, called of "Undershot," his mill being driven by a wheel, the working power of which is hidden unheeded by him, to break out some day to the damage of both his mill and him.

Pococurantism:[†] Indifference, nonchalance.

Poor-Law Bastilles:[†] The unpleasant workhouse to which paupers were sent as a result of the Poor Law of 1834. The goal of this law was to discourage any but the truly desperate to seek help.

Potosi: An important mining and commercial town of Bolivia, situated 13,000 ft. above sea-level on the slopes of the Cerro de Potosi; is one of the loftiest inhabited places on the globe, but a dilapidated, squalid place. There is a cathedral, next to Lima the finest in South America, a mint, and extensive reservoirs; the streets are steep and without vehicles; the climate is cold, and the surrounding hillsides barren; the industry is silver mining, but the mines are becoming exhausted and flooded.

Present Time: Defined impressively by Carlyle as "the youngest born of Eternity, child and heir of all the past times, with their good and evil, and parent of all the future with new questions and significance," on the right or wrong understanding of which depend the issues of life or death to us all, the sphinx riddle given to all of us to

---

18 From Gibb, A. D., *Legal Terms* (1946).

rede as we would live and not die.

Pusey, Edward Bouverie:† Leading figure in the Oxford Movement, a movement to reintroduce older Christian traditions—mostly Catholic—into Anglican practice.

Puseyism: Defined by Carlyle to be "a noisy theoretic demonstration and laudation of *the* Church, instead of some unnoisy, unconscious, but *practical*, total, heart-and-soul demonstration of *a* Church, ... a matter to strike one dumb," and apropos to which he asks pertinently, "if there is no atmosphere, what will it serve a man to demonstrate the excellence of lungs?"

Pym, John: Puritan statesman, born in Somersetshire, educated at Oxford; bred to law, entered Parliament in 1621, opposed the arbitrary measures of the king, took a prominent part in the impeachment of Buckingham; at the opening of the Long Parliament procured the impeachment of the Earl of Strafford, and conducted the proceedings against him; he was one of the five members illegally arrested by Charles I, and was brought back again in triumph to Westminster; was appointed Lieutenant of the Ordnance, and a month after died (1584-1643).

Rack-Rent, Grace Of Castle:† The landlord of Castle Rackrent, of the eponymous 1800 novel by Maria Edgeworth.

Rate In Aid:[19] The Rate-in-Aid Act [...] provided additional funds for the Poor Law through a 6d in the pound levy on all rateable properties in Ireland.

Ready-Reckoner:[20] A table of numbers used to facilitate simple calculations, esp. one for applying rates of discount, interest, charging, etc, to different sums.

Red Republicans: A party in France who, at the time of the Revolution of 1848, aimed at a reorganisation of the State on a general partition of Property.

Repeal Agitation: Agitation by the Repeal Association,[21] an Irish mass membership political movement set up by

---

19 From Kinealy, Christine, *This Great Calamity: The Irish Famine 1845–52* (1994).
20 From *Collins English Dictionary*, retrieved 2021.
21 From *Wikipedia*, retrieved 2021.

Daniel O'Connell in 1830 to campaign for a repeal of the Acts of Union of 1800 between Great Britain and Ireland.

Reforming Pope: Pius IX.[22] In the [...] two years from 1846-1848, from his election as pope to his escape to Gaeta, Pope Mastai appeared to be a liberal and enlightened sovereign, a champion of the prospective Risorgimento.

Revolt of Three Days: Carlyle's reference to the July Revolution,[23] insurrection that brought Louis-Philippe to the throne of France. The revolution was precipitated by Charles X's publication (July 26) of restrictive ordinances contrary to the spirit of the Charter of 1814. Protests and demonstrations were followed by three days of fighting (July 27–29), the abdication of Charles X (August 2), and the proclamation of Louis-Philippe as "king of the French" (August 9).

Sansculottes: [i.e. fellows without breeches], a name of contempt applied by the aristocratic party in France to the Revolutionists, and at length accepted by the latter as a term of honour, as men who asserted their claim to regard on their naked manhood.

Sansculottism: Belief in the rights of man, stript of all the conventional vestures and badges by which alone, and without any other ground of right, one man maintains an ascendency over another.

Sauerteig: [i.e. leaven], an imaginary authority alive to the "celestial infernal" fermentation that goes on in the world, who has an eye specially to the evil elements at work, and to whose opinion Carlyle frequently appeals in his condemnatory verdict on sublunary things.

Sedan and Huddersfield:[24] Towns (the first French, the second English) where wool was woven.

Silence, Worship of: Carlyle's name for the sacred respect for restraint in speech till "thought has silently matured itself ... to hold one's tongue till *some* meaning lie behind

---

22 From *Catholic Culture Library*, retrieved 2021.
23 From *Britannica*, retrieved 2021.
24 From *The Broadview Anthology of British Literature*, vol. 5 (1962).

to set it wagging," a doctrine which many misunderstand, almost wilfully, it would seem; silence being to him the very womb out of which all great things are born.

Sincerity: In Carlyle's ethics the one test of all worth in a human being, that he really with his whole soul means what he is saying and doing, and is courageously ready to front time and eternity on the stake.

Smelfungus: A name given by Sterne to Smollett as author of volume of *Travels Through France and Italy*, for the snarling abuse he heaps on the institutions and customs of the countries he visited; a name Carlyle assumes when he has any seriously severe criticisms to offer on things particularly that have gone or are going to the bad.

Solecism: The name given to a violation of the syntax or idiom of a language, as well as to an incarnate absurdity of any kind, whether in mind or morals.

Sorrow, Worship of: Goethe's name for the Christian religion, "our highest religion, for the Son of Man," Carlyle adds, interpreting this, "there is no noble crown, well worn or even ill worn, but is a crown of thorns."

St. Ives: (1) A town in Cornwall, 8 m. N. of Penzance, the inhabitants of which are chiefly engaged in the pilchard fisheries. (2) A town in Huntingdonshire, on the Ouse, 5 m. E. of Huntingdon, where Cromwell lived and Theodore Watts the artist was born.

Strauss, David Friedrich: German theological and biblical critic [...] made his name known over the whole theological world; this was his *Leben Jesu*, the first volume of which appeared that year, in which he maintained that, while the life of Christ had a historical basis, all the supernatural element in it and the accounts of it were simply and purely mythical, and the fruit of the idea of His person as Divine which at the foundation of the Christian religion took possession of the mind of the Church [...] his last work was entitled *Der Alte und der Neue Glaube*, in which he openly repudiates the Christian religion, and assigns the sovereign authority in spiritual matters to science and its handmaid art.

Stulz (Stultz), George:† A premier tailor for men's clothing

Glossary

in Regency England, tailor to Beau Brummel.

Stump Orator: One who is ready to take up any question of the day, usually a political one, and harangue upon it from any platform offhand; the class, the whole merely a talking one, form the subject, in a pretty wide reference, of one of Carlyle's scathing *Latter-Day Pamphlets*.

St. Vitus:[†] Patron saint of dancers, whose name is given to Sydenham's chorea as "St. Vitus Dance", a neurological disorder causing uncoordinated and involuntary spasms. Carlyle uses this as metaphor for knee-jerk and ill-considered actions.

Sumptuary Laws: Passed in various lands and ages to restrict excess in dress, food, and luxuries generally; are to be found in the codes of Solon, Julius Caesar, and other ancient rulers; Charles VI of France restricted dinners to one soup and two other dishes; appear at various times in English statutes down to the 16th century against the use of "costly meats," furs, silks, &c., by those unable to afford them; were issued by the Scottish Parliament against the extravagance of ladies in the matter of dress to relieve "the puir gentlemen their husbands and fathers"; were repealed in England in the reign of James I; at no time were they carefully observed.

Surplice Controversy:[†] Any of a series of disputes from the 16th through the 19th centuries over the use of Roman Catholic vestments in post-Reformation England and America.

Taillefer:[†] A Norman poet (name lit. "iron cutter"), who at the battle of Hastings sang the *Chanson de Roland* at English troops, was rushed by a soldier whom he killed, and charged the English lines.

Tailors: Carlyle's humorsome name in *Sartor* for the architects of the customs and costumes woven for human wear by society, the inventors of our spiritual toggery, the truly *poetic* class.

Talapoin:[25] A Buddhist monk or priest.

Talfourd-Mahon:[†] Thomas Noon Talfourd and Lord Ma-

---

25 From *Wiktionary*, retrieved 2021.

Turgot, Anne Robert Jacques: French statesman, born at Paris, of Norman descent; early embraced the doctrines of the *philosophe* party, and held for 13 years the post of intendant of Limoges, the affairs of which he administered with ability, and was in 1774 called by Louis XVI to the management of the national finances, which he proceeded to do on economical principles, but in all his efforts was thwarted by the privileged classes, and in some 20 months was compelled to resign and leave the matter to the fates, he himself retiring into private life (1727-1781).

Twelfth Hour of the Night:[†] Dawn, 6 A.M.

Ugolingo Della Gherardesca:[†] Italian nobleman, depicted in Canto XXXIII of Dante's Inferno as starving in a tower prison cell with his children.

Valetism:[26] All heroes will be flawed. Their heroism lay in their creative energy in the face of these difficulties, not in their moral perfection. To sneer at such a person for their failings is the philosophy of those who seek comfort in the conventional. Carlyle called this 'valetism', from the expression 'no man is a hero to his valet'.

Weissnichtwo: (Know-not-where), in Carlyle's *Sartor*, an imaginary European city, viewed as the focus, and as exhibiting the operation, of all the influences for good and evil of the time we live in, described in terms which characterised city life in the first quarter of the 19th century; so universal appeared the spiritual forces at work in society at that time that it was impossible to say *where* they were and *where* they were *not*, and hence the name of the city, Know-not-where.

---

26 From *Wikipedia*, retrieved 2021.

Studies in Reaction Series:

I	Jonathan Bowden	**Why I Am Not a Liberal**
II	Thomas Carlyle	**The Present Time**
III	George Fitzhugh	**Sociology for the South**
IV	Henry Sumner Maine	**Popular Government**
V	Aristotle	**Essays on Endoxa**
VI	Numa Denis Fustel de Coulanges	**The Ancient Family**
VII		**Havamal**
VIII	Joseph de Maistre	**The Generative Principle of Political Consitutions**
IX	Robert Filmer	**Patriarcha**
X	Jean Bodin	**On Sovereignty**
XI	Livy	**Ab Urbe Condita, Book I**
XII		**The Wanderer and Other Old English Poetry**
XIII	Oswald Spengler	**Prussianism and Socialism**
XIV	Theodore Kaczynski	**Industrial Society and its Future**

www.ingramcontent.com/pod-product-compliance
Lightning Source LLC
Chambersburg PA
CBHW021150080526
44588CB00008B/282